over ... I atten ... on crea ... Christian retreat center just west of Cincinatti. There were Christian scientists in attendance from all over the world - geologists, an astronomy professor from U. of South Carolina, and many others who spoke. One of the most fascinating speakers was Dr. Werner Gitt, a German information scientist and the author of the book. He has discovered natural laws that relate to information. Some of his conclusions, based on these natural laws pertaining to information, are that neither macro-evolution (molecules to man evolution) nor the Big Bang could ever have occurred.

In this book he has written some very interesting and pertinent (to us) thoughts about time and eternity - thoughts worth pondering.

Ron

To my loved ones

Werner Gitt

Time and Eternity

Loizeaux
Neptune, New Jersey

dⳑv
Christliche
Literatur-Verbreitung e.V.

About the author: Prof. Dr Werner Gitt was born in Raineck, East Prussia in 1937. From 1963-1968 he obtained his engineering degree (Dipl.-Ing.) at the Technical University of Hanover. Thereafter he worked as an assistant at the Institute of Control Engineering at the Technical University of Aachen. Following two years of research work he received his doctorate *summa cum laude*, together with the prestigious Borchers Medal from the Technical University of Aachen, Germany, in 1970. He is now a Director and Professor at the German Federal Institute of Physics and Technology (Physikalisch-Technische Bundesanstalt Braunschweig). He has written numerous scientific papers in the field of information science, numerical mathematics and control engineering, as well as several popular books, some of which have been translated into Bulgarian, Chinese, Czech, French, Hungarian, Italian, Polish, Roumanian, Russian, Spain, and other languages. In 1990 he founded the specialist conference in Information Science which 150 participants attend every year. The aim of this meeting is to combine biblical guidelines with ideas from information science. Since 1984 he has been a regular guest lecturer at the State Independent Theological University of Basle, Switzerland, on the subject ›Bible and Science‹. He has held lectures on related topics at numerous universities at home and abroad, as well as having spoken on the topic ›Faith and Science‹ in a number of different countries (e.g. Australia, Austria, France, Hungary, Kazakhstan, Kirghizia, Namibia, New Zealand, Poland, Portugal, Roumania, Russia, South Africa, and the USA).

First English Edition 2001

© of the German Edition:
Werner Gitt, »Zeit und Ewigkeit«
1999 by CLV • Christliche Literatur-Verbreitung e. V.
Postfach 11 01 35 • D-33661 Bielefeld, Germany

© of the English Edition:
2001 by CLV • Christliche Literatur-Verbreitung e. V.
P.O. Box 11 01 35 • D-33661 Bielefeld, Germany
Translation: Dr Carl Wieland, Brigitte Stoll
Cover: Dieter Otten, Gummersbach
Typography: CLV
Printed in Germany: by Ebner Ulm

ISBN 0-87213-228-5 (Loizeaux)
ISBN 3-89397-473-3 (CLV)

Contents

Translators' note: re Bible versions.

Bible verses were often translated directly from the German in an effort to ensure maximum clarity within the author's context, while keeping to the meaning of the original Hebrew or Greek. At other times, to achieve this goal, an existing English translation, such as the Authorized Version or the New International Version, was utilized in whole or in part.

Foreword

The Problem of Time: People from the most diverse of centuries have pondered the phenomenon of time, without coming to an adequate explanation of it. *Augustine* (354-430) said, »What is time? If no one asks me, I know; but if any person should require me to tell him, I cannot.«

One and a half millennia later, the English philosopher and mathematician *Alfred North Whitehead* (1861-1947) had nothing but his own frustration to add to *Augustine's* bewilderment: »It is impossible to contemplate time... without being overcome by the sense of how limited human intelligence is.«

The Australian professor of mathematical physics and the philosophy of science at the University of Adelaide, *Paul Davies*, wrote in the foreword of his book »About Time« [D1, pp. 9-10]: »Fascination with the riddle of time is as old as human thought. The earliest written records betray confusion and anxiety over the nature of time. ...The orthodox account of time frequently leaves us stranded, surrounded by a welter of puzzles and paradoxes.«

And it is not just the nature of time which presents a puzzle for thinkers – its origin is just as problematic. Like most – but by no means all – of his contemporaries, *Davies* proceeds from the Big Bang theory, but finds no answer there either for the origin of time [D1, p. 18]: »Today, the big-bang [has become the orthodox cosmology. It] nevertheless faces a major hurdle in providing a convincing account of how the universe can come to exist from nothing as a result of a physical process. No greater obstacle lies in the path of explanation than the mystery of how time itself can originate naturally. Can science ever encompass the beginning of time within its scope?«

Even *Einstein's* relativity theory has not brought about the hoped-for breakthrough [D1, p. 34]: »The revolution started by Einstein remains unfinished. We still await a complete understanding of the nature of time.«

Why is something as fundamental as time so difficult to comprehend and so hard to explain? The psychologist *John Cohen* says: »We are here confronted by a deep mystery, in the truest sense of the word – one which on the one hand lies at the heart of human experience, on the other in the nature of things.«

The challenge of this book: The above statements clearly show that only a completely new approach to the problem of »time« can help us further. We accept this challenge, in order to arrive at our goal via a new way of thinking. The phenomenon of time is of such supreme significance for our lives, that I believe a renewed analysis is definitely overdue.

We will first consider time as a purely physical quantity. Describing time from this aspect is in keeping with the observation of the Japanese philosopher *Masanao Toda* [D1, p. 274]: »No one, apparently, can claim to know what time is. Nevertheless, there is this brave breed of people called physicists, who used this elusive notion as one of the basic building blocks of their theory, and miraculously, the theory worked.«

Only then do we come to the main part of this book, in which we deal with time in a central and novel way as an anthropological [Greek: *anthropos* = man] quantity. Finally, the third part of this book deals with the issue of what awaits us beyond time: eternity.

Advice to readers: This book has been written for a wide, general audience. In my view, parts II and III are the most important. These may be read without necessarily first working through part I, the physics section.

Thanks: The contents of this volume were discussing in considerable detail with my wife, after which the manuscript was reviewed by the language professional *Dörte Götz*. Their numerous comments and suggested amendments led to improvements in the book's contents, or to making these more readily accessible. I am very grateful to both for their committed co-labours.

Werner Gitt

Additional foreword to the English edition

As the author, I am of course delighted that this book, having been translated into Hungarian and Polish, has now also appeared in English, joining the seven other of my titles available in that language.

I want to say a very special ›thank you‹ to my Australian friend *Carl Wieland* and his sister *Brigitte Stoll*, who translated this book in its entirety. They achieved more than a stylistically excellent result, as with the translation of a novel; due to *Carl's* wide scientific knowledge and their deep Biblical understanding, they were able to add to the book here and there to improve the end result.

Dr Wieland is the director of the world-renowed organisation for creation science/research, *Answers in Genesis* in Brisbane (Australia). He is the editor of their brilliantly presented and colourful English-language magazine Creation (print run > 50,000) which has subscribers in more than 140 countries.

Werner Gitt, June 2001

I: Time – a physical quantity

1.1 The International System (SI[1]) of measurement for physical quantities

In the world of science and technology, measuring units such as mile, pint, horsepower, calorie, etc. have long since been relegated to a bygone age. They have been replaced by the easily handled SI system,[2] which does away with

---

[1] The international system of units (Système International d'Unites), which carries the universal abbreviation SI in all languages, was introduced in 1960 at the *11th General Conference on Weights and Measures* [French: *Conférence Générale des Poids et Mesures (CGPM);* Committee with representatives from the Metre Convention member states. First conference in 1889. Meeting every 4th year. Approves the SI-System and results from fundamental metrological research]. It ended a confusion of over a century caused by a multiplicity of units and unitary systems. The SI was developed by various international expert committees of measurement, in which the following institutions took part on behalf of the Federal Republic of Germany: the Federal Institute of Physics and Technology (Physikalisch-Technische Bundesanstalt or PTB) and the German Institute for Standardization (Deutsches Institut für Normung, or DIN). In international unitary systems a distinction is made between *fundamental* and *derived* units.

[2] The effectiveness of the SI system can be demonstrated using a difficult example. The unit of **magnetic flux density** derives from voltage × time/area: 1 Vs/m^2. Expanding the fraction by multiplying top and bottom line by 1 ampere (A), we get 1 VAs/Am^2. VA = W (watts, after the Scotsman *James Watt* (1736–1819) who invented an efficient steam engine), so this becomes 1 Ws/Am^2. Substituting now for 1 Ws $= 1 \text{ kgm}^2/\text{s}^2$ (see units of energy, p. 15) we arrive at $1 \text{ kgm}^2/\text{Am}^2\text{s}^2 = 1 \text{ kg/As}^2$. Thus the magnetic flux density has been expressed using only the fundamental units listed in the main text: $1 \text{ kg}/(\text{A} \times \text{s}^2) = 1 \text{ T } (= 1 \text{ tesla})$. This is equal to the surface density of a homogenous magnetic field of the strength of 1 weber (Wb), which perpendicularly penetrates all points of a surface of 1 m^2. Here the unit is named after the American physicist *Nikola Tesla* (1856–1943) who in 1881 developed the principle of the rotating field electric motor (three-phase AC

complicated conversion factors. All conceivable physical
units can be derived from a basic system of seven fundamental quantities which are independent of each other
— one of these being *time*.

· Length   (Unit: metre, m)
· Mass   (Unit: kilogram, kg)
· Current strength (Unit: ampere, A)
· Temperature   (Unit: kelvin, K)
· Substance amount (Unit: mole, mol)
· Light intensity   (Unit: candela, cd)
· **Time**   (Unit: second, s)

For each of these **fundamental units** there is an unambig-
uous, internationally established physical definition [X1].
All units known to us (and any yet to be formulated) relating to the material world are inevitably derived from some
of these fundamental units, interconnected via multipli-
cation and division. Units are often named after an internationally known physicist.

It is important to note that the full name of the unit is not
capitalised, even if it is named after someone. Abbreviations
of units are not usually capitalised unless they are named
after someone. And there is never an abbreviation point or
a plural ›s‹ after an abbreviated unit. For example, ice melts
at 273.15 kelvins or 273.15 K, and a fuse wire may be designed
to melt with a current over five amperes (›amps‹) or 5 A.

Whenever the resulting unit becomes too unwieldy or un-

---

motor) and in 1887 described the multiphase system for the transmission of electrical power. The field strength unit is named after German physicist *Wilhelm Weber* (1804–1891).

sightly, it is given a new name with a corresponding abbreviation. We can see this from some examples of derived units.

Velocity (speed in a given direction) is equal to distance/time; from this, it follows that its unit is metre/second = m/s.

Because of the relationship (Newton's Second Law of Motion): Force = mass × acceleration ($F = m \cdot a$), it follows that the unit of **force** is 1 kg·m/s^2 (acceleration = metres per second per second, or m/s^2). This new unit of force is named after the English physicist *Isaac Newton* (1642–1727), who is regarded as the founder of classical theoretical physics: 1 N (= 1 newton) = 1 kg·m/s^2.

Energy (mechanical) is calculated as force × distance (in the direction of the force); it follows that its unit is 1 (kg·m/s^2) · m = 1 kg·m^2/s^2 = 1 J. The unit J (= 1 joule = 1 Nm = 1 Ws) is named after the English physicist *James Prescott Joule* (1818–1889), who determined the thermal equivalent of mechanical and electrical energy.

Returning, then, to time.

1.2 The unit of time

The **physical unit of time** is the **second**. This was previously defined as 1/86,400[th] of a mean solar day. However, the mean solar day[3] is not constant; currently its du-

---

[3] **The division of time:** The choice of a day as a measure of time was a logical connection to a universally known natural phenomenon. However, the division of a day into two lots of 12 hours, and then dividing these again into 60 minutes, each of 60 seconds, was purely arbitrary. It would have been much more convenient to have introduced the tried

ration is increasing by 1.8 milliseconds (1 ms = 0.001 s) per century.[4] So this definition of a second became inadequate for modern-day requirements. To overcome this dilemma, a new definition of a second was internationally adopted at the *13th General Conference on Weights and Measures* in 1967. A second henceforth is:

9,192,631,770 times

the duration of one period of oscillation at the characteristic ›vibrational frequency‹ of an atom of cesium-133.[5]

---

and tested decimal system here also. There is no natural law which would indicate that, as a unit of time, the second has any inherent advantages, or is likely to be especially useful in everyday practice. Thus the establishment of the duration of a second also rests on a purely arbitrary choice.

The clock of the Strasbourg (Straßburg) Cathedral: Among the many clocks constructed over the centuries, one in particular deserves special mention: the Strasbourg Cathedral clock. By decree of the council of Nicea (AD 325), the date of Easter falls on the first Sunday after the first full moon following the beginning of Spring (March 21st). Can a mechanical device indicate such an intricately established date? Built and rebuilt several times over the past 600 years (with the last major rebuild in 1842), the clock of the Strasbourg Cathedral achieves this and much more; this unique and amazing device functions as an astronomical and calendrical computer. Among its achievements; calculating sidereal time, lunar time and solar time, with an error of less than a second a century, and tracking the motion of 5,000 stars. Fully Y2K compliant (including all the complex conventions for tracking leap years) over two lifetimes ago, one of its marvellous conglomeration of gears is designed to turn only once in a century; another once in 2,500 years.

[4] According to the *Encyclopaedia Britannica*, in 1956 the International Conference on Weights and Measures defined a second as 1/31,556,925.9747 of the length of the seasonal (tropical) year 1900, and ratified this in 1960. But since 1900 was in the past, there was no way reproduce it.

[5] This nuclide of cesium, ^{133}Cs, is the only one that occurs in nature.

In fact, the atom does not really vibrate, it is the characteristic frequency of the radiation absorbed when an electron jumps between two hyperfine levels of the cesium atom's ground state. This duration is established with the help of cesium atomic clocks.

So the second has become chopped into more than 9 billion[6] parts, each corresponding to a physical process! The number was chosen to match the length of the second to the 1965/1906 definition. The measurement of time thus becomes the counting of certain sequentially occurring events. This definition allows the unit of time to be reproduced at any time, and any place, given the appropriate equipment.

1.3 Measuring time with atomic clocks

At the Federal Institute of Physics and Technology in Braunschweig (Brunswick), Germany, are found two of the world's most accurate cesium atomic clocks [B1]. In regard to their degree of accuracy, these clocks, CS1 and CS2, are at the global cutting edge. CS2 (see **figure 1**) has been operational since 1985, and runs so accurately, that in a theoretical two million years hence (should there still be an earth then, and were this instrument to last that long) it would differ by at most only 1 second from an ideal clock. That corresponds to a relative uncertainty[7] of only

---

[6] This book will use the U.S. convention for large numbers, in which one billion = a thousand million (10^9), and one trillion = a thousand billion, or a million million (10^{12}).

[7] Relative uncertainty: This figure is derived by dividing the possible error in time measurement ($\Delta t = 1$s) by the time period under consideration ($t = 2$ million years): $\Delta t/t = 1\text{s}/6.3 \times 10^{13}\text{s} = 1.6 \times 10^{-14}$. Applied to a day that would be 1.4 nanoseconds.

$1.6 \cdot 10^{-14}$. Such a value for its functional accuracy does not come from comparing it with another clock — because there is no such ideal clock. It is done via a calculated estimate of the effects of all the participating parameters of the clock CS2.

The cesium-133 (^{133}Cs) utilized in atomic clocks is not radio-active; it is stable, and has the remarkable property of melting at the comparatively low temperature of 28 degrees Celsius, and boiling at 690 °C. Simplified, what happens inside an atomic clock is as follows: A beam of free cesium atoms is produced. They are passed through a very strong magnetic field, so that they all find themselves in one of two possible energy states, and are bathed in microwaves in a resonator (based on electromagnetic oscillations). Through this influence, the energy state of the atoms changes, and they switch over to the previously unoccupied energy state when the microwave photon energy $h \times \nu$ is exactly the same as the energy difference between the two hyperfine levels. During this transition from one to the other state, the atoms either emit (Latin *emittere* = to send out, to give out) or absorb (Latin *absorbere* = to swallow, to devour) electromagnetic waves with a very specific frequency, which may be regarded as a natural constant.

This thus establishes the quantum mechanical »norm« of the frequency, which forms the basis for the »exact time«. What is then needed is to build an apparatus, i.e. an atomic clock, with which this natural frequency can be measured with great certainty and high precision. For reasons of measuring technology, this is best done when the interaction time between the cesium atoms and the microwave radiation is as long as possible. This in turn comes from using the slowest possible atoms.

Figure 1: *The cesium atomic clock C2 at the Federal Institute of Physics and Technology, Braunschweig (Brunswick), Germany.*

In the primary clock CS2 (and also CS3), the ray tube is horizontal, in CS4 it is vertical. The latest development, the fountain clock [CSF1; **Ce**Sium **F**ountain clock no. **1**], utilizes a method for which *Steven Chu, Claude Cohen-Tannoudji* and *William Phillips* were awarded the Nobel Prize for Physics in 1997. With the help of laser light, they succeeded in cooling atoms to an extremely low temperature, just a few microkelvins (mK) above absolute zero (-273.15 degrees Celsius), trapping them, like a swarm of bees, as a cloud of a few million atoms. Within such a magneto-optical trap, atoms normally impelled by the ambient temperature into a furious zig-zag pace move at a leisurely speed of only a few millimetres per second. If now the frequency of the laser light is briefly put »out of tune«, these cooled and trapped atoms receive an upwards kick. They leap up at 4 m/s, rising until gravity has »used up« their energy of motion, then they fall back down again. This scenario is reminiscent of a fountain, hence the name »fountain clock«.

Just as in a conventional atomic clock, the source atoms are prepared in one or another energy state. They switch their energy state when they pass the microwave field of a resonator during their up-and-down motion. But the time they have in contact with the microwave field is significantly greater: a stone thrown up one metre takes about a second to hit the ground. The atoms in the fountain clock are in contact with the microwave field for about the same amount of time, which is why the measured resonance signal is correspondingly sharper.

With this new development, the goal of fixing the duration of a second with even greater precision is now within reach. After construction is completed, the accuracy anticipated is of such a high order that the relative uncertainty would be only 10^{-15} seconds. Such a clock would be »out« by at most one second in over 10 million years.

Time is the physical quantity which can be measured with the highest precision of all. Is such ultra-precision necessary? The following will clarify this in relation to navigation on the earth's surface.

1.4 De termining position with the aid of precise time measurements

a) The fervent to determine longitude

For shipping on the open ocean, current position is of crucial significance. If you know the degree of latitude and longitude of a ship at sea, this unambiguously fixes its position. While latitude can be determined with the help of the stars [G3, pp. 92–97], there is no corresponding method for obtaining longitude. Before the GPS method (see part (b)) became available, position could only be determined by utilizing the distance travelled. This distance s is a product of the velocity v and the travel-time t ($s = v \cdot t$), so v and t have to be continually measured. Locating one's position on the ocean thus required accurate time measurement. Not having appropriate clocks (i.e. both seaworthy and sufficiently accurate) at sea will not only mean arriving at the wrong destination, it can be life-threatening. Two significant historical occurrences are worth mentioning in this connection [B2, p. 155]:

· **In 1691**, the English fleet lost several ships, because the aforementioned navigation methods employed by their captains were too inaccurate. One simply no longer knew where one was on the ocean.

· **In 1707**, there was a worse tragedy. A squadron of ships coming from the direction of Gibraltar, under way for twelve days, thought that it was off the shore of Brittany when, on the foggy night of 22nd October, it ran aground on the rocks of the Scilly isles, west of Cornwall. The losses were grave: 2,000 men and four ships.

In those days, one tried to sail in the vicinity of a visible coastline where possible, because navigators had no way of determining longitude. In literally hundreds of cases, ships went down because once at sea, there was no way to determine the degree of longitude. Attempts were made to ascertain geographical position using the speed of the ship and the travel time. Had there been really accurate clocks, a ship's position on the open sea could have been calculated, but as it was, crude estimates had to suffice.

The American science reporter *Dava Sobel* gave her important and gripping book, »Longitude« [S2], the subtitle: »The true story of a lone genius who solved the greatest scientific problem of his time.« In it she wrote [S2, pp. 7-8]:

»The active quest for a solution to the problem of longitude persisted over four centuries and across the whole continent of Europe. Most crowned heads of state eventually played a part in the longitude story, notably *George III* and *Louis XIV*. Seafaring men such as Captain *William Bligh* of the *Bounty* and the great circumnavigator Captain James Cook, who made three long voyages of exploration and experimentation before his violent death in Hawaii, took the more promising methods to sea to test their accuracy and practicability. Renowned astronomers approached the longitude challenge by appealing to the clockwork universe: *Galileo Galilei, Jean Dominique Cassini, Christiaan Huygens, Sir Isaac Newton*, and *Edmond Halley*, of comet fame, all entreated the moon and stars for help. Palatial observatories were founded at Paris, London, and Berlin for the express purpose of determining longitude by the heavens. … As time passed and no method proved successful, the search for a solution to the longitude problem assumed legendary proportions, on a par with discovering the Fountain of Youth, the secret of perpetual motion, or the formula for transforming lead into gold. The governments of the great maritime nations — including Spain, the Netherlands, and certain city-states of Italy — periodically roiled the fervor by offering jackpot purses for a workable method.«

In 1717 the British Parliament, desperate to overcome this

predicament, offered a very large prize. The winner would be whoever could invent and construct *a clock usable at sea*. The three prizes set out in the »Longitude Act« depended on the level of accuracy with which geographical longitude could be established.

- 10,000 pounds sterling for 1 degree of longitude (1°)
- 15,000 pounds for 40 minutes of a degree of longitude and
- 20,000 pounds for half a degree (30 minutes).

In today's terms, these were several millions of dollars. Considering that half a degree of longitude at the equator is nevertheless still a difference of 56 kilometres, the accuracy demanded appears rather modest.

A young man named *John Harrison* (1693–1776) took up this challenge. He began working on the solution to this problem at the age of 21.

- His **first clock** weighed 35 kg.
- The **second**, finished in 1739, weighed 50 kg.
- The **third** took a few more years, but even this one was not yet satisfactory.
- Finally, in **1759**, the **fourth clock**, which met the requirements for accuracy, was finished. *Harrison* wrote of it, that there was no more splendid mechanical or mathematical instrument in the world.

The crucial test at sea came in 1761, during a voyage from Portsmouth to Jamaica. At the stopover port of Madeira the clock had its first test. While the captain fancied himself to be 13° 50' west of Greenwich, according to the clock it was 15° 19' — and the clock was right, as the arrival in Porto Santo the next morning confirmed.

It was only in the year 1772 — 11 years after that stunningly successful test voyage — that *Harrison* finally received his well-earned prize. In the meantime, he had become 79 years old, receiving the reward for his life's work after decades of political intrigues, feuds, academic libels, scientific revolutions and economic upheavals.

This lengthy struggle over longitude determination shows just how vitally significant the measurement of time is for the purpose of determining position. Today, from any place on earth, we can determine our position in a few seconds, to within a metre – only because of the highly precise measurement of time with atomic clocks.

b) Determining position with the help of GPS

Nowadays, on the basis of very exact measurements of time, it is possible to fix accurately, to the metre, the position of ships on the ocean, or explorers in the desert. This is done via the »Global Positioning System« (GPS). 24 artificial satellites orbit the earth. Four at a time move in unison along one of six orbital paths, beaming their signals to earth. The orbits have been chosen such that at any time, the signals from at least four satellites can be utilized by a GPS receiver from any point worldwide. On board each satellite, there are four atomic clocks. The geographic location of the receiver is calculated from the differences in transit time of the signals from several satellites. These differences are very precisely measurable to within a few nanoseconds.

Another example: The space probe *Voyager 1*, having covered around two billion kilometres in its three year journey through our planetary system, was due to beam pictures of Titan, Saturn's largest moon, back to Earth. Remarkably, the target destination, as had been calculated in advance, was missed by only 19 km. A time error of only a thousandth of a second would have resulted in the probe straying off course by hundreds of kilometres.

1.5 Shortest and longest time-span

The **shortest time-span** that physicists have ever been able to measure is the life-time of certain rare elementary particles, which last for only the trillionth part of a billionth of a second. Half of the atomic nuclei of the helium isotope of mass 5 (^{5}He) — each one five times as heavy as the nucleus of a hydrogen atom — decay in the unimaginably short time of $2 \cdot 10^{-21}$ s. This number has a zero in front of the decimal point, and then only after another 20 zeros is there the number two:

0.000 000 000 000 000 000 002 seconds.

Or, alternatively: $2 \cdot 10^{-12} \cdot 10^{-9}$ seconds: expressed in words, that would be two trillionths of a billionth of a second!

The longest time-span measurable is the time which has elapsed since the creation of this universe. The Heidelberg astrophysicist and director of the Königsstuhl observatory, Prof. *Heinrich Vogt* (1890 – 1968) said:

»The entire cosmos — space and the matter contained therein — is bounded by time. Time itself began with the origin of the cosmos. Whatever there was before the ›beginning of time‹ is out of the reach of scientific research. At that point, the space-time world accessible to science merges into a spaceless, timeless realm, one which the intellect of man is unable to grasp, and which remains for him an eternally unfathomable, divine mystery.«

1.6 Time constants and periods

a) Time constants and oscillation periods in physics.

In physics, various reproducible processes are of differing duration. The *oscillation period* T is referred to in the case of periodic events, or the *time constant* T for non-periodic ones. (In a first order reaction, like nuclear decay, the amount of material $N(t)$ remaining at time t with an initial amount N_0 is given by $N(t) = N_0 \cdot e^{-t/T}$. The half-life ($\tau$) is related to the time constant T by $\tau = T \cdot \ln 2$). Let's look at some physical constants:

The half-life of helium-5 (^{5}He): $\tau = 2 \cdot 10^{21}$ s

The half-life of uranium-235 (^{235}U): $\tau = 700$ million years. (Note: A half-life has nothing to do with age!)

Oscillation period of a pendulum of length $L = 20$ m:
$T = 2 \cdot \pi \cdot \mathrm{SQRT}(L/g) = 8.97$ s where Earth's gravitational acceleration $g = 9.81$ m/s^2
$T \cong 9$ seconds

Oscillation period of a pendulum of length $L = 1$ m:
$T = 2.006$ s $\cong 2$ seconds

The oscillation period of a 440 Hz tone (= the musical note A) has a period:
$T = 1/f = 0.00227$ s $\cong 2\,\frac{1}{4}$ thousandths of a second = $2\,\frac{1}{4}$ ms

›Oscillation period‹ T of a ^{133}Cs atom (actually the oscillation period of the electromagnetic radiation corresponding to one particular electronic transition):

Frequency f = 9,192,631,770 Hz (it is an integer number)
(1 Hertz = 1 Hz = 1/s = 1 oscillation per second)
Oscillation period $T = 1/f = 108.78 \cdot 10^{-12}$ s
$T \cong 100$ trillionths of a second = 100 ps

The wavelengths of visible light lie between 380 and 780 nm (1 nm = 10^{-9} m = 1 billionth of a metre). For green light of wavelength λ = 540 nm, the oscillation period can be calculated as follows:

$f = v/\lambda; v = c$ = 299,792,458 m/s
(the speed of light in a vacuum; it is an integer number)
$T = 1/f = \lambda/v$ = 540 nm/299,792,458 m/s = $1.8 \cdot 10^{-15}$ s
$T \cong 2$ quadrillionths of a second = 2 femtoseconds (fs)
= 2 millionths of a nanosecond (ns)

The oscillation period of visible light is thus five thousand times shorter than that of the characteristic radiation involved in cesium atomic clocks.

Similarly, there are time constants in many other fields of science and technology, such as e.g. astronomy, biology and chemistry:

b) Times in astronomy [G3]

- The fastest known pulsar (PSR 1937+214) has a period T = 0.001558 s or 1½ ms (thousandths of a second).
- 1 sidereal day on Earth: T = 23 h 56 min 4.09 s (= the duration of the earth's rotation around its own axis relative to the ›fixed‹ stars — the sidereal rotation period).
- 1 Mercury year: 88 Earth days (the exact value of this sidereal orbit time: 87.97 days).
- 1 Mercury day: 58.646 Earth days (sidereal rotation time). A peculiarity: On Mercury, one solar day or the synodic period (= the time between two identical so-

lar positions, e.g. from high noon to high noon) on
Mercury is exactly twice as long as a Mercury year, be-
cause 58.646/(87.97-58.646) = 2
- One Jupiter year: 11.862 Earth years
- One Jupiter day: 9h 50 min 30 s (the fastest axial rota-
  tion in our planetary system)

c) Time in biological systems

Whereas the time constants of physics and astronomy can
be given very precisely, biological time constants and processes, by comparison, have a wide scatter.
We live 70 times as long as the smallest mammal, the
shrew, and 1200 times as long as a fly. Reaction times
also differ greatly. When we try to catch a fly, we notice
how it is able to instantly react. Its eyes can perceive very
small time intervals. It can react to a pouncing hand in
less than a hundredth of a second. Our own reaction time
is a tenth of a second.

Birds, too, are capable of perceiving much smaller time
intervals than we are. We hear the variety-rich songs of
many birds as a smooth melody. If we record these on
tape and play them back at a slower speed, we can hear
significantly more details than in a »live« concert. Sounds
which are in reality interrupted by very small time intervals are perceived by us as continuous. By contrast, birds
can distinguish, as individual tones, a string of sounds
which are separated from each other by intervals as minute as only two milliseconds or less.

The pace of life: In vertebrates, i.e. animals with a back-
bone, the frequency of heartbeat is a good measure of
their natural »rhythm«, or their physiological pace of life.
On average, vertebrates take one breath for every 3.9

heartbeats. Remarkably, most organisms with a reasonably long life-span experience, on average, the same number of heartbeats during their lifetime, namely 800 million. This natural physiological rhythm or pace in birds and mammals depends (among other things) upon their body size. It is increased in smaller mammals, which have a faster heart rate, and a higher metabolic rate. For larger mammals, the situation is the reverse.

The smallest mammal, the tiny shrew, has a life which is 30 times faster than an elephant's. For a shrew, 24 hours are so long that it divides this period into many smaller intervals of activity and rest. Within one rotation of the earth, it experiences several »shrew-days«. A shrew's heart beats around 1,000 times per minute (period of each beat cycle = 0.06 s), that of an elephant only 30 times (period = 2 s), and that of a whale 15 times (period: 4 s). Shrews live at most one and a half years, whereas elephants can live to 50 years or more.

Our perception of time: We know from our own experience that in childhood, the days appear to pass slowly, accelerating with advancing age. At birth, our heart races at 140 beats per minute, which sinks to 70 per minute in adulthood. The associated changes in metabolic rate influence our physiological pace of life accordingly.

1.7 Other aspects of physical time

1. The direction of time's arrow: The course of events in our world, as is conspicuously obvious to all, flows in one direction. We talk about the irreversibility of occurrences. Time appears to us to be directed, as if provided with an arrow that points from the past into the future. We human beings experience ourselves as being in the current of time, which sweeps us irrevocably from birth to death.

A cup knocked off the table shatters into many pieces. No matter how long we sit and wait for it to happen, the pieces will never rearrange themselves back into a cup which then leaps back up onto the table. Nothing like this ever happens. Throw a stone into a pond, and ripples form on the water surface, spreading out as concentric waves from the entry point. The mathematical equation describing this process also has a solution in which time runs backwards, i.e. all the ripples flow from the shore back to a central point, then disappear as a stone rises from the water. Yet obviously, this process — such as one would see in a film played backwards — never occurs in nature.

This leads to the question of whether this arrow of time, which for us only has one direction, can be given a physical basis. In fact, there is a physical law which sets out a direction to time. According to the Second Law of Thermodynamics, *entropy* can be defined as a physical quantity. In contrast to familiar and measurable quantities such as temperature or electrical current strength, entropy is a physically unobservable, yet nevertheless mathematically calculable quantity. The Second Law is a natural law which specifies among other things that in an ideal isolated system (i.e. one in which neither matter nor energy is exchanged with its surroundings) the entropy relentlessly increases with time. This gives us a physical basis for the uni-directionality of time's arrow.

2. The relativity of time: The Theory of Relativity is the inclusive term for two theories about the nature of space and time[8] put forward by *Albert Einstein* (1879-1955). Few insights in the natural sciences have brought about such revolutionary changes as has Einsteinian relativity. Newtonian mechanics, in which time and space are seen as absolute quantities, has been subsumed by relativity into a wider, more generalised system. The time-honoured physics of Newton allows us to describe processes in which all the events take place at velocities which, in comparison to that of light, are low.

According to relativity theory, time's arrow does not move with constant speed, but is dependent on the velocity of the system. The relativistic time dilation of a clock depends on its velocity v relative to a clock in a system at rest. Just how tiny this time dilation is, even in unusual Earth-conditions, is shown by the following experiment. In 1971, a cesium atomic clock spent 15 hours on board an aeroplane flying at 278 m/s (= 1000 km/h). Afterwards, the time it showed lagged behind an identical clock on earth by $4.7 \cdot 10^{-8}$ s. This time shortening corresponded to the time dilation (Lat. *dilatio* = delay; here used in the sense of slowing down the passage of time when measured by an external observer) expected according to *Einstein*. Relativistic effects become significant when the velocities involved reach an appreciable percentage of the speed of light (as in e.g. atomic physics, astronomy). The life-spans of short-lived elementary particles measured by an outside observer can substantially increase when these travel at close to the velocity of light.

As far as our life on earth is concerned, the effects of rela-

---

[8] Known as the special and general theories of relativity, respectively.

tivity on time are so minute as to be totally insignificant. So following this brief discussion, we will leave it there.

From a physical viewpoint, we know quite well what time is. As the ongoing research into the development of new atomic clocks shows, the precision with which time can be measured is being continually improved. Even the physical characteristics of time have been comprehensively researched. The renowned American physicist and 1965 Nobel prize winner *Richard P. Feynman* (1918–1988) said that the time for discovery in this realm is virtually past [F1, p. 172]: »The age in which we live is the age in which we are discovering the fundamental laws of nature, and that day will never come again.« But time is more than physics! — and that is the subject of the part which follows.

Time units: The following lists some common time units and their conversions factors:

1 year (Latin *annus*) = 1 a = 365 d = 8,760 h = 31,536,000 s
1 day (Latin *dies*) =1 d = 24 h = 86,400 s
1 hour (Latin *hora*) = 1 h = 60 min = 3,600 s
1 minute (Latin *minutus*) = 1 min = 60 s
1 second = 1 s = 1000 ms
1 millisecond = 1 ms = 10^{-3} s = 1000 ms
   (= 1 thousandth of a second)
1 microsecond = 1 ms = 10^{-6} s = 1000 ns
   (= 1 millionth of a second)
1 nanosecond = 1 ns = 10^{-9} s = 1000 ps
   (= 1 billionth of a second)
1 picosecond = 1 ps = 10^{-12} s = 1000 fs
   (= 1 trillionth of a second)
1 femtosecond = 1 fs = 10^{-15} s
   (= 1 quadrillionth of a second)

II: Time – an anthropological quantity

The heading poses the central question: what is the nature of time for us humans?

2.1 Introduction

At this point we will let a quotation from *Erwin Schrödinger* (1887-1961), Nobel prizewinner for physics in 1933, introduce an aspect of time that transcends the realm of physics. Time affects us in a very personal way. *Schrödinger* said: »For time is truly our severest master, in that it forces the existence of each one of us into tight boundaries – 70 to 80 years, as written in Psalm 90.« Where can we best obtain the meaning of time for our lives? In a physics textbook? From the philosophers? From the psychologists? Along with various other inapplicable concepts, the Greek philosophers taught that time and its related events were recurrent in nature, turning like a giant wheel. Whilst philosophy and psychology can provide many helpful stimuli for our thinking, their insights are not far-reaching enough to give us a final, definitive answer.

No human being can adequately describe for us the actual nature of time. If we want to find this out in a way which is firmly based and lastingly relevant, we must ask the One who made time. Many authors agree that time did not always exist. Time only came into existence at the creation of the universe. Time was created together with space and matter. As a consequence, we must turn to the Creator if we want to discover more than can be measured with mere physical instruments. In His book, the Bible, He has given us ample relevant information.

From the Bible we learn that there is no eternal cycle of
things, but that the time available to us is unique. Furthermore, it has a beginning as well as an end. In one of
the oldest parts of the Bible – the book of Job – we find
that time is a measure which is determined and allotted
to us by God: »Man born of woman is of few days. ...
He springs up like a flower and withers away; like a fleeting shadow he does not endure. Man's days are determined; you have decreed the number of his months and
have set limits he cannot exceed« (Job 14:1-2,5).

This thought is taken up by Jesus in the New Testament:
»Which of you by worrying can add a single hour to his
life?« (Matthew.6:27). This rhetorical question from the
Sermon on the Mount has a very short answer: No one!
It is good to bear this characteristic of time in mind. A
certain amount of time is allotted to each one of us. Jesus' statement is precise; we cannot extend our life, but
we can shorten it. By our manner of living, particularly as
regards nicotine, alcohol, drugs, poor diet, we can – as
medical authorities confirm – cut short the quantum of
life-span allotted to us, but no one can add anything to it.
Friedrich von Bodelschwingh (1831-1910) once said pertinently: »Everything which reminds us that time has an
end is of benefit.« The Bible does not direct our thoughts
toward the past, but toward the present and the future.
We are to shape our life according to our goal, our destination, which is also why Psalm 90:12 says: »Teach us to
number our days aright, that we may gain a heart of wisdom.« I have adopted the following motto for myself:

»Today I want to use my time in such a way that five
minutes after my death I will be able to say that that is
how I wanted to utilize it.«

2.2 Attributes of Time

Time has several conspicuous attributes which we will consider a little more closely:

1. Time cannot be stored: In our computers we can store enormous amounts of data which can be retrieved at any given time in the future. This is impossible to do with time. Unused time is irretrievably lost. We cannot say to any moment in time: »Stay but, thou art so fair!« as *Goethe* says in his Faust. Likewise that other advice of the poet: »Take hold of the moment and forestall it!« is not realizable.

2. Time cannot be lent out: A housewife can borrow sugar and salt from her neighbour and return it at any time, but with time that is not possible. Thus a Russian saying pertinently observes: »Time cannot be loaned for a while!« Each person lives out their own time. We can lend out money and goods, but we cannot do this with time.

3. Each day has the same amount of time: The day of the American President and that of the German Chancellor each has the same 24 hours as your day and mine. Here there is no distinction. This can be graphically imagined: We are all seated on a **conveyor belt** and strapped to it firmly and immovably with a wide strap. We all travel at the same speed on this conveyor belt of time. Nobody can overtake anyone else, but at the same time we cannot lag behind. The conveyor belt binds us all; it sets our boundaries for us. Only God does not sit on the conveyor belt; nor is He strapped to it. He can survey the entire belt at a glance. With Him, a thousand years are as one day (Psalm 90:4), but also one day as a thousand years (2 Peter 3:8).

4. Time cannot be skipped: Some would like to skip over a portion of the axis of time, or insert a pause. Utopians have offered thoughts on the subject:

a) Time machine: The novelist *Herbert G. Wells* (1866-1946) wrote the novel »The Time Machine« (1895). In 1960 it was turned into a movie which today counts as one of the classics of science fiction. It tells the story of an English inventor named George who, on New Year's Eve 1899, presents his friends with a machine in which one can travel through time. In the movie George actually sets out on such a journey. His machine can travel into the future, and also return. Depending on the position of the lever, he can race through the ages at differing speed settings:

- A candle burns out in seconds.
- The shadow on the sundial turns in a flash.
- The starry sky rotates at phenomenal speed.
- The sun moves across the sky by day like a rapidly passing lamp.
- Whole years, too, are traversed at breakneck speed.
- It is possible to halt the time machine and then experience a segment of the future in real-time.
- Finally he moves so far into the future, that totally different beings live in his home area.
- At last he returns with his time machine to the place and time from which he set out – and everything is back to how it was.

This kind of thing is only possible in science fiction, but not on our time axis, which we can only traverse continuously and in one direction.

b) Suspended Animation: The Hungarian-German-American physicist *Leo Szillard* (1898-1964) dedicated two brilliantly written stories to the subject of the split lifetime. In »The Voice of the Dolphins« a Dr. Jones is reawakened after 18 years of cryogenic »sleep«, when a remedy has been found for his cancer illness. Before going into his cryogenic sleep, Dr. Jones gives a remarkable farewell party for his friends [B1, pp. 184-185]: »Most of them probably somehow had the feeling that they were experiencing *my* funeral, since they would never see me alive again; to me, on the other hand, it seemed as if it were *their* funeral, as at the time of my return to life they would no longer be alive.«

c) **Cryogenics:** In California there is a firm called AL-COR, directed by Mr. *Thomas Donaldsen*, that enables people to be frozen in liquid nitrogen at –196°C. A dozen doctors are involved with the preparations for deep freezing: the blood is extracted from the body and replaced by a kind of anti-freeze solution. Quite a number of people have in recent times availed themselves of this extremely expensive form of storage (TV report June 1990).

> I do not believe that these people will ever return to this life. Man consists of **spirit, soul** and **body**, and all these experiments are carried out only on the biological part of man, the material part. No one can freeze or preserve the soul.

5. **Time earns no interest when invested:** *F.L. Boschke*, the former editor-in-chief of the magazine »Natural Sciences«, writes [B1, pp. 206 & 218]: »Almost all errors and mistakes that we make can be corrected, but we can never make up one lost day – ever. Spent lifetime is spent, nowhere do we get a credit or even just interest on our allotment of time.«

It would be a great bonus if we could obtain credit for time we've spent in travel or waiting, time we wasted or did not use, and so gain access to this time again in order to be able to use it better the second time around. The older we become, the more the time allotted to us shrinks, until there is only a scant remnant at the twilight of life. Who would not then wish for a time-account in which the hours wasted through sleep, day-dreaming or unprofitable waiting had accumulated and from which we could then withdraw these saved-up deposits of time? No one has ever been able to save up such a credit of time. We are helplessly subject to the march of time. We cannot influence the passing of time. The author and journalist *Claus Gaedemann* (1928-1995) writes: »Time – every hour, every day, is our life, our only capital, unable to be increased, the raw material of our existence, which is being relentlessly consumed.«

6. Time is progressive; the arrow of time has a definite direction: A film can be wound backwards, but never time. Time always marches on in one direction. The former French President *François Mitterand* (1916-1996) had a principle in regard to his time. He said: »I never wear a watch, watches are whips for all those who allow themselves to be misused as racehorses.« Even though he did not wear a watch, the timepieces on the wrists of his attendants were all the more accurate. No one gets around the passing of time.

7. Events in our world involve the consumption of time: Every physical process and all completed events require a certain amount of time[9] for their execution. Worldwide,

---

[9] In contrast to the events of our experience, the miracles of God/ Jesus took place without involving any consumption of time.

in a single second, on average the following takes place (1999 statistics):

- 4.5 cars are manufactured
- 2,000 m² of forest are wiped out
- three people are born
- 1.5 people die
- the mountain of debt of the German Republic grows by DM 3935
- globally, 12.6 million m³ of water fall as precipitation, and 3.2 million m³ of that fall on dry land

Further events of one second's duration:

- the Concorde covers 611 metres
- the Space Shuttle flies 7.7 kilometres
- on its orbit around the sun, our planet travels 30 kilometres
- the Amazon, the river with the greatest volume of water in the world, carries 120,000 m³ of water into the Atlantic (by comparison: the mouth of the Danube 6240 m³; the Rhine 2330 m³; figures refer to rise values in each case)
- 2.4 million red blood-cells are produced in our bone marrow [K2, p. 46]
- our lungs require 200 cm³ of air [K2, p. 72]
- 4 billion impulses are exchanged between the cortical hemispheres in our brain [K2, p. 148]

Each process takes its necessary amount of time to transpire, and the many events in the life of a person take place at their appointed time. For all these things »there is a time«, as is so pertinently recorded in Ecclesiastes 3:1-15:

»There is a time for everything,
and a season for every activity under heaven:

a time to be born, and a time to die,
a time to plant and a time to uproot,
a time to kill and a time to heal,
a time to tear down and a time to build,
a time to weep and a time to laugh,
a time to mourn and a time to dance,
a time to scatter stones and a time to gather them,
a time to embrace and a time to refrain,
a time to search and a time to give up,
a time to keep and a time to throw away,
a time to tear and a time to mend,
a time to be silent and a time to speak,
a time to love and a time to hate,
a time for war and a time for peace.
What does the worker gain from his toil?
I have seen the burden God has laid on men.
He has made everything beautiful in its time.
He has also set eternity in the hearts of men;
yet they cannot fathom what God has done
from beginning to end.
I know that there is nothing better for men
than to be happy and do good while they live.
That everyone may eat and drink,
and find satisfaction in all his toil
– this is the gift of God.
I know that everything God does will endure forever;
nothing can be added to it and nothing taken from it.
God does it so that men will revere him.
Whatever is has already been,
and what will be has been before;
and God will call the past to account.«

Two noteworthy words are used at the outset of our Bible
text: »everything« and »every«. They serve to emphasize

the point that nothing, but absolutely nothing, that happens in this world, and especially in our personal lives, is excluded from the strict passage of time in accordance with the laws of nature. Everything requires its time, but by the same token, all events and experiences – irrespective of whether we would rate them as good or bad – only last a certain time. The list of activities given above, together with their opposites, seeks to express that nothing is exempted from the chronological expiration of time, the tarrying on that conveyor-belt of time. We could augment the list at will with excerpts and events from our own lives:

There is a time for childhood,
a time for youth,
a time for adulthood;
a time to be single and a time to be married;
a time to have friends and a time to be deserted by friends;
a time to be healthy and a time to be sick;
a time to be rested and a time to be weary;
a time to be patient and a time to be impatient;
a time to be satisfied and a time to lament and complain;
a time to be happy and a time to be depressed;
a time to pray and a time to wait for how and when God will answer.

We experience periodically recurring events like joy and sorrow, being hungry and being satisfied, but also things that only occur once. For me the terrible events of the war were incisive; flight, expulsion, my mother being forcibly taken away, and the many times death threatened. We are glad that bad events have limits to »their time«, and then are over. Whereas we would like to retain beautiful things forever. Whilst this is not possible, folk and popular songs pick up this theme nonetheless, with a longing look backwards: »If only we could be twenty again,« or »Youth is wonderful, it comes but once«. In this world, God has ordained the temporal state, so it is appropriate for us not to look back with sadness or nostalgia, but to give thanks for what we have been given. Giving thanks is also appropriate for those things which have caused us toil and trouble (Ephesians 5:20), for they, too, were only temporal, and do not last.

In the framework of world history, numerous unique events also have their immovable place on the time axis: the discovery of America by *Christopher Columbus* (1492), the Reformation through *Martin Luther* (1521), the discovery of X-rays by *Wilhelm Conrad Röntgen* (1895), the first heart transplant operation by *Christian Barnard* (1967), or the first landing of a man on the moon by *Neil A. Armstrong* (1969).

In Ecclesiastes 3 God points beyond everything temporal: »Everything that God does will endure forever«. If we are seeking things lasting and eternal, we have been given a firm foundation for this quest, on which we can build what will never perish: »For no one can lay any foundation other than the one already laid, which is Jesus Christ. If any man builds on this foundation … . If what he has built survives, he will receive his reward.« (1 Corinthians 3:11-14).

2.3 Two biblical concepts of time: kairos *and* chronos

When the Bible speaks of time, it does so primarily in relation to questions of man's significance and existence. It distinguishes between two essentially different kinds of time, denoted in the Greek New Testament by the terms *chronos* and *kairos.* This verbal distinction exists neither in English nor in most other languages. Wrong conclusions, with far-reaching consequences, have therefore often been arrived at in the area of biblical interpretation, because in regarding these two concepts as equivalent, their essential difference has been ignored.

2.3.1 Chronos: *the time of man*

Chronos is time which is physically measurable (see Part I) and so refers to the historically transpiring time of chronology. A strict lawfulness underlies it, one by which we humans, too, are bound. For us, day, month and year have become the measure of this concept and classification of time. The North German pastor and evangelist *Heinrich Kemner* (1903-1993) characterized it thus [K1, S.29]: »*Chronos* describes time as the sum of the moments of a linear movement in space and time.« This expresses an essential truth: time cannot be separated from space and matter. **Time**, **space** and **matter** make up the basic physical substance of this world, and none can be examined in isolation from the others. In the creation of which we are a part this *chronos* can be defined in terms of natural law. Time is coupled to matter, so when matter was created out of nothing (Hebrews 11:3), time also came into existence. As in **figure 2**, we will call this zero on the time axis $t_{beginning}$. The axis of time has a defined starting point. It is a linear (i.e. an axis of equidistant scale) and one-dimensional (i.e. a continuous axis with only one co-ordinate) phenomenon. Chronological time is marked by the fact that it is constantly progressive and only runs in one direction. It is impossible for us either to turn it around or to repeat it. We speak of the »river of time«. Our present moment in time lies somewhere on this axis. Strictly speaking, the present (the »now«) has no duration. Everything lying beyond this moment we call the past, and that which lies ahead of us, the future. The question arises as to whether the time axis has a future limitation, or whether it is endless. Here the answer the Bible gives is both clear and unequivocal:

Matthew 24:35 – »Heaven and earth will pass away.«
1 Corinthians 7:31 – »This world in its present form is passing away.«
1 Peter 4:7 – »The end of all things is near.«

These words forcibly draw to our attention that this world is marked for demolition. If, however, this world and its material content are limited then, because of the above-mentioned coupling of space, matter and time, the latter must also be subject to a limitation. This is in fact exactly what the Bible tells us in Revelation 10:6 »There should be time no more«. Thus the chronological future is not limitless, but has a measure predetermined by God, which in **figure 2** is given as t_{end}. The Bible is the only book that gives us the history of mankind from beginning to end in one mighty sweep. No other source of information has such a vast scope.

Somewhere along this time axis, we can mark off the span of our life. Our time neither runs in a circle nor repeats itself. It runs forwards, and happens but once, uniquely unrepeatable and in strict measure between birth and death. We experience time differently from the way we experience space; we can enter a given part of space as often as we choose. We can presumably revisit the *place* of our childhood again and again, but we can never return to the *time* of our childhood. Time is the big One-way Street of our life.

2.3.2 Kairos: *God's time*

The Bavarian theologian *Hermann Bezzel* (1861-1917) re-
marked on the limited environment of our being with the
words: »Space and time have about them and within them
an enslaving and restrictive effect.« In character and nature completely different and free from all the familiar
and limiting qualities of *chronos* is the *kairos* of God.
»God's clock« does not measure in seconds, hours and
years, because it is not tied to the restrictions of space
and matter: »Are your days like those of a mortal or your
years like those of a man?« (Job 10:5). The *kairos* of God
is fulfilled time in which confining concepts like past and
future no longer have a place. In **figure 2**, therefore, *kairos* is shown as outside and above our time axis. God is
spirit, and as Lord of creation is not confined by the phenomena of time and space which He created. God sees
and overlooks the entire time axis at a single glance, so
for Him various time segments on our time axis do not
represent realms through which one still needs to pass.
God encompasses 1,000 years with the same glance as He
does any particular day. For this reason, that which at
first seems inconceivable to us is true of God: »For a thousand years in your sight are like a day that has just gone
by, or like a watch in the night« (Psalm 90:4). Unfortunately this text is often incorrectly used to interpret into the
creation account in Genesis 1 an evolution with long time-
spans. I must strenuously warn against this practice. Those
who would handle God's Word in this manner would, to
be consistent, need to apply the above text from the psalm
to Matthew 27:63, which would give them the sentence:
»After 3,000 years I will rise again.« If that were the intended meaning, we would still be waiting for Jesus' re-
surrection today. But He is alive – He is risen! We must

not manipulate the word of the Bible according to our
wishful thinking, but must carefully heed this God-given
information.   According to the testimony of the Bible,
when, with the creation of matter (Genesis 1:1), time was
also created, the rest of the work of creation took place in
a strict chronological sequence of day-night cycles. The
measuring system for this is described in Genesis 1:14 –
»Let there be lights in the expanse of the sky to separate
the day from the night, and let them serve as signs to mark
seasons and days and years.« This is the earliest, and therefore oldest, method of measuring time, which therewith
clearly consigns the creation process to *chronos*. I.e., the
creation took place in six days of »our« time.

The question as to whether God's time and man's time
can be converted into one another is fully answered for us
if we also consult 2 Peter 3:8 – »But do not forget this one
thing, dear friends: With the Lord a day is like a thousand years, and a thousand years are like a day.« Written
in equation form, this means:

   1 God-day = 1,000 man-years
   1,000 God-years = 1 man-day

The conclusion is obvious:

There is no conversion formula for *kairos* into *chronos*
and vice-versa.

Kairos and *chronos* differ from each other not only on the
question of scale, but more especially that of **quality** and
dimension. Consideration of these features will guard us
against a superficial interpretation of the Bible. The higher dimension of the *kairos* of God, as against *chronos,* al-

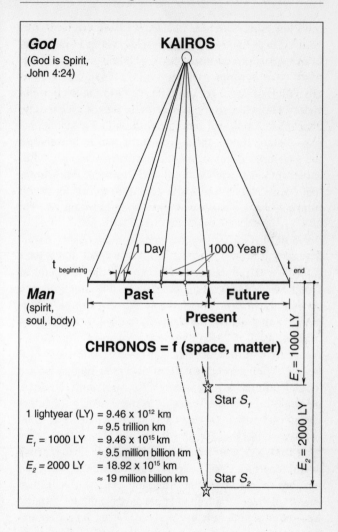

Figure 2: *Toward an understanding of the nature of time. The difference between man's time (chronos), and God's time (kairos).*

ways becomes evident at the point where God declares Himself as the One who sovereignly acts in space and time. Thus God can speak of already-concluded processes, although for us in *chronos* they are still in the future. Before the nation of Israel goes into battle, God can declare the victory He will give them over their foes as an already-concluded action: »I *have given* them into your hands« (e.g. Joshua 10:8). In the prophetic text of Revelation the grammatical tense is noticeably often changed. Because of God's independence of our *chronos*, He can relate events, which for us still belong to the realm of the future, as having happened and having been settled.

According to God's creation ordnance, man consists of spirit, soul and body. Because we have a spirit that comes from God (Ecclesiastes 12:7), man has that attribute of God's which enables him to relativize the time axis in a certain manner. Let us imagine ourselves to be at this moment on a star S1 (see **figure 2**) that is 1,000 light-years from the earth. The light-year is a measure of distance and is defined by the distance that light covers in one year, which is 9.46 trillion kilometres. If we now imagine that we are looking through an appropriate telescope from S1 to earth, we could become eyewitnesses to those events which occurred on earth 1,000 years ago. From a star S2 at 2,000 light-years' distance from earth, we would have the opportunity of taking a backward look along the time axis which would lead to a 2,000 year-old past. Similarly, we could imagine an exact position in the universe from which we could watch the Children of Israel crossing the Red Sea. If we – even though only in the power of our imagination – can transport ourselves into a situation which allows us to experience a certain contemporaneousness of all past events, how much more does this then apply to God?

Therefore we can picture the *kairos* of God as eternal contemporaneousness, annulling the immutable principle of sequence of our chronological time-flow.

2.4 The five levels of information – a new basis for interpreting time

In a world shaped by science and technology, we are confronted by information at every turn: in the systems of modern computer technology, in communications technology, in natural and artificial languages as well as in all biological systems.

The American communications scientist *Claude E. Shannon* (1916-2001) was the first to attempt to quantify information. **Shannon's Theory of Information**, named after him, deals with the statistical aspect of a sequence of symbols (e.g., the number of symbols in a sequence of letters). Actually, this theory disregards the meaning contained within the sequence of symbols, and is therefore unsuited to covering all aspects of information. The statistical quantity of information is measured in bits.

In order to overcome the restrictions mentioned above, I have developed the **Natural-Law Theory of Information**, which was first called this in [G6], and which is marked by the following points [G4, p. 155]:

·   Scientific derivation: Just as all laws of nature are arrived at through observation of known systems, so the various theorems about information are also derived from observation.
·   All laws of nature so far known to us relate exclusively to matter. By way of extending this, theorems relating

- to information were formulated which also have the efficacy and applicability of natural law.
· Just as laws of nature can always be successfully applied to unknown cases, so the theorems of information also permit reliable conclusions in such cases.
· Laws of nature are not limited to certain fields or applications, because according to all our present knowledge they are universally valid. The same also applies to the theorems of information. They are thus equally valid for living and non-living systems.
· A clearly delineated zone of definition can be specified [G4, p. 159 and G6, p. 207], which permits a sharp dividing-line to be drawn between systems within or outside of this domain.

Only by broadening the statistical understanding of information through addition of the further aspects of syntax, semantics, pragmatics and apobetics is the concept of information in all its fullness given due consideration. In my book »In the Beginning was Information« [G1] I introduced this concept at length. This novel concept of information is based upon an extremely important and fundamental fact, namely that this quantity represents not a material but essentially a spiritual phenomenon. Whilst information may be stored on matter and transferred by means of physical systems, it in no way originates in purely material processes, but always through an ideas-giver, that is, through employment of intelligence and will. In the materialistic theories this fact is ignored, because information is assumed to be a purely physical phenomenon.

Figure 3 graphically portrays everything that is required for information. Here we see clearly that a sender and a recipient are mandatory for all information. Apobetics

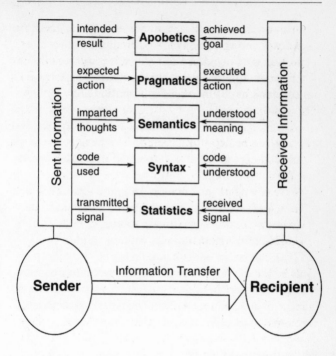

Figure 3. *The five-level concept of the Natural-Law Theory of Information.*
It is true of any encoded information that it is sent out by someone (sender) and directed to someone (recipient). Essentially five different levels can be distinguished. The highest level, that of apobetics, concerns the goal or result of information. Pragmatics, the next level down, records the action intended to be caused. One step lower deals with the meaning intended to be understood (semantics). The second-lowest level involves the linguistic encoding/decoding of thoughts and the last level deals with the technical concept of transmission, and the associated statistical data. All five aspects have their specific distinguishing characteristics for both sender and recipient. The individual levels are all interdependent. The information goal has not been achieved if a premature break occurs at any of the lower levels.

(Greek *apobeinon* = goal, result, outcome), as the fifth
level, is a necessary part. When examining unknown cases,
it can always be decided whether one is within or outside
of the zone of definition of information. The most important **laws of nature about information** are as follows
[G1, p. 80]:

- There can be no information without a code.
- Any code is the result of a free and deliberate agree-
  ment/convention.
- There can be no information without a sender.
- There can be no chain of information without an intel-
  ligent instigator as its ultimate source.
- There can be no information without volition (will).
- There can be no information unless all five hierarchi-
  cal levels are involved: statistics, syntax, semantics,
  pragmatics, apobetics.
- Information cannot originate in statistical (stochastic,
  random) processes.

The information theory briefly described here is further
unfolded, substantiated and discussed in greater detail in
[G1], using numerous examples. This Natural-Law Theory
of Information enables far-reaching conclusions to be
drawn – provided one is within the domain of definition –
even to the point of asking questions about the origin of
life. Life is to a large degree determined by information,
and because of these natural laws this information demands an intelligent source. The idea of evolution, that
information in matter is supposed to have arisen spontaneously, is therefore false from the outset.

The five-level concept of information can also be derived
from the Bible [G1, pp. 134-168]. This is a salient exam-

ple, showing that study of the Bible enables recognition of important structures and interconnections of reality, which we would otherwise hardly have stumbled upon. The Bible also throws totally new light on scientifically »unintelligible« phenomena.

Time: During my investigations of the concept of »time« I noticed something unexpected: even though **information** and **time** are totally different phenomena, a remarkable analogy exists between the two: the five-level concept of information [G1] can, surprisingly, also be applied to time. The question thus arises as to whether comparable natural laws exist for the different levels of time as can be derived for information.

What follows is a detailed explanation of the **five-level concept of time.**

2.5 The five levels of time

As will now be demonstrated in detail, human time may be represented, in analogy to the five-level concept of information, as a five-level concept of time. By way of numerous Bible passages and graphic examples from life, this new approach to the phenomenon of time will be demonstrated and substantiated. There is a multitude of biblical propositions which can be allocated precisely to one of the five levels of time, whereas others by reason of their breadth can span two or even three levels.

2.5.1 Statistics of Time

Measuring statistical time: For the physicist time is, as a measurable entity, nothing but a measure of quantity without any aspect of quality. All clocks – from the hourglass to the atomic clock – record only its statistical aspect. On this statistical level we humans are only concerned with the measure of available time, with the time span of our lives, the number of our years. In analogy to information, this is the equivalent to the length of a chain of symbols, i.e. the sequence of alphabet letters. The Bible tells of the *oldest method of measuring statistical time* in Genesis 1:14 – »Let there be lights in the expanse of the sky to separate the day from the night, and let them serve as signs to mark seasons and days and years«. Measurement occurs here with the aid of the heavenly bodies. The sundial is mentioned in 2 Kings 20:9 as a measuring instrument. Time during the night was divided into four equal segments, the so-called night watches (Matthew 14:25).

The brevity of our time: The Bible repeatedly points out the brevity of our life-span, using fleeting events from nature such as wind, shadows and vapour to make the point:

Wind: »My days are swifter than a weaver's shuttle, and they come to an end without hope. Remember, O God, that my life is but a breath« (Job 7:6-7). The wind blows only for a certain time, then it is gone. It is only of a momentary nature. With this comparative illustration the Bible points us to the transience of our fleeting life.

Shadow: »Man is like a breath; his days are like a fleeting shadow« (Psalm 144:4). The shadow of a tree depends on the position of the sun, and takes its path from the sun's course. Should a cloud suddenly move across the sky, the shadow is no more. Or picture an express train, rapidly crossing the landscape. Wherever it happens to be at any given moment, its shadow will be visible. Just as its shadow races away from the onlooker, so our earthly time also fades away.

Vapour: »What is your life? You are a mist that appears for a little while and then vanishes« (James 4:14). When water boils we see the steam trails rise. But the steam is not visible for long before it dissolves into the surrounding air and becomes invisible. This picture also graphically describes our brief earthly existence.

The Bible contains many other statements, using ever new words and turns of phrase, concerning the brevity of our life. What follows is only a selection:

Job 14:1,5 – »Man born of woman is of few days ... Man's days are determined; you have decreed the number of his months and have set limits he cannot exceed.«

Psalm 39:5 – »You have made my days a mere handbreadth; the span of my years is *as nothing* before you.«

Psalm 89:47 – »Remember how fleeting is my life.«

1 Chronicles 29:15 – »We are strangers before you, and sojourners ... our days on earth are like a shadow, and there is no hope or expectation of remaining.«

Many a person is fascinated by the lifestyles of famous people. They, too, were well aware of the brief span of their lives. However, the conclusions that many of them drew from this are by no means exemplary, because their life was characterized solely by the here and now. Their thinking lacked any reference to eternity.

Romy Schneider (1938-1982): She became well-known through three »Sissi« films (1955-1957), in which she played the young Empress of Austria and so became the darling of the German cinema-going public of the 50s. Although known world-wide, she strove tirelessly for further fame. It was her ambitious plan to become the greatest actress of our time. She lived her life in line with the following motto [S1]: »Who knows how long luck will last, I live only for the moment.« — »It is better to have a short and beautiful life, than a long and temperate one.« She never gained a grip on her life. She was married twice, but never found happiness. Alcohol and pills provided no solution. In 1982, at the age of 44, she took her own life.

Curt Jürgens (1915-1982): He belonged to the small number of German actors who could rightly call themselves a »world-famous star.« He acted in more than 100 international films, partnering *Brigitte Bardot* or *Danny Kaye*, as a dashing swordsman, a gravelly-voiced chevalier or a laughing vagabond. In Germany he gained popularity mainly through a military role: in the film version of *Carl Zuckmayer's* resistance drama »The Devil's General« he played the recalcitrant ace-pilot Harras. From *Jürgens* comes the following statement, in which he turns his mind to the question of time as it affects his own life: »It is more important to add more life to your years, than more years to your life.« However, at the end of his life he was overtaken by the fear of death: »Sometimes I do think that I should perhaps have lived a different life. Then I am overcome with fear of dying, and have my doubts whether it was right not to believe in God.«

Nina Ruge (1957-): She studied biology for a teaching career in high school, but in a TV interview (21 May 1999) declared that she did not want, at this point in her life, to be able to predict that in her sixtieth year of life, at 1:30 p.m. in the afternoon, the last lesson she would take would be over.

So she decided to become a journalist and TV moderator. She realizes how transient life is and has determined: »I want to taste this short life to the fullest.« At 42 years of age she already has two broken marriages behind her.

2.5.2 Syntax of Time

Just as there is a syntax[10] (rules of grammar and style) for natural and artificial languages, so this applies also to time, whereby we here refer to the rules for making use of time: What strategies do we use for optimal time-planning? What concepts and rules for creating deadlines will allow us an effective use of time? How do we avoid hectic schedules and stress? How do we construct a program for our life?

Thanks to mobile phones, lap-top computers and e-mail, the performance-oriented manager is able to make himself available in the evenings, on weekends and on the now customary short holidays. In the USA a fashionable term has already been coined for them: »IT-victims« (victims of Information Technology) – the term used for all those who spend 24 hours a day, seven days a week, in the service of the firm, and who are never able to switch off and unwind. In the midst of this electronic high-achievement network people become isolated; dialogue and person-to-person contacts are neglected. The constant lack of time becomes an ongoing problem. Time management appears to be the solution to the problem, and so

---

[10] **Regarding syntax:** divergent from conventional language science, within the framework of the Natural-Law Information Theory, grammar and theory of style are still counted as belonging to the level of syntax, even though they can be employed as semantic means of expression.

numerous firms hold appropriate seminars for their stress-
ed managers, which are run by high-earning consultants.
In his essay, *Marcel Mettler* names eight golden rules of
time management [M1, p. 32] which are helpful, but which
– as we will yet see – are still limited in their grasp of the
syntactical aspect of time:

1. Give up perfectionism. Don't allow unimportant details to deter you from the essentials.
2. Steer discussions and conferences. Determine discussion goals and prepare notes well in advance.
3. Avoid working without a plan. Set goals for the day
   and check at night whether you have achieved them.
4. Don't aim to do everything yourself. Delegate where
   this is sensible.
5. Don't do many things simultaneously. Determine pri-
   orities.
6. Don't wish to know everything. Trust others and leave
   details to them.
7. Finish unpleasant and started tasks first. Don't allow
   unimportant telephone messages and callers to keep
   you from your work.
8. Take each matter to hand only once, and then deal with
   it speedily and smoothly.

Anyone wanting to observe the night sky will see more
with binoculars than with the naked eye. Distant galaxies
and astronomical details will, however, remain beyond the
reach of the observer. Modern reflecting telescopes, on
the other hand, open up whole new and undreamt-of
realms. In the same way, methods of time management
certainly have their place, but their reach stops far too
short, because they are limited to the purely earthly realm.
If in this sense we want to employ »far-reaching reflect-

ing telescopes« we need to ask the Bible for its recommended time-syntax. The Bible names criteria, which help us to a time management of a completely different kind.

1. First biblical syntax-rule of time: The first rule of this kind is found in the Ten Commandments: »Six days you shall labour and do all your work; but the seventh day ... on it you shall not do any work« (Exodus 20:9-10).

During the time of the French Revolution, the Calendar of the Revolution was introduced (from 22nd September 1793), in which each month was divided into three decades of 10 days each. The year was made up of twelve months at 30 days each + 5 days, or 6 days in a leap year. The new calendar was meant to free the memory of the people of all things Christian and encourage in its place the internalizing of agriculture as a political foundation. The months were named accordingly: after Vendemiaire (grape-harvest month) came Brumaire (month of fog), Frimaire (month of frost), Nivose (snow month), Pluviose (rain month) and Germinal (month of germination). The creator of the calendar, *Fabre d'Eglantine,* lived only long enough to experience his calendar twice, because he died on the 14th Germinal (5th April 1794) by the guillotine. The arbitrarily introduced 10-day rhythm did not prove a success because from the Creation we have been designed for the 7-day rhythm – as it is practised right around the world. *Napoleon* abolished the Calendar of the Revolution on 1st January 1806.

On a lecture tour in Kazakhstan in May 1992, we were welcomed by the Lord Mayor of the city of Karaganda. He complained about his workload: »I sleep four hours a day. Sundays don't even exist for me.« I don't know how long he will be able to keep that up.

2. Time-syntax according to the Sermon on the Mount:
In the Sermon on the Mount Jesus names another very
important rule for the use of time. Although the word
»time« does not even occur in the verse, we nonetheless
find here a very foundational directive for handling time:
»Seek first the kingdom of God and his righteousness, and
all these things will be given to you as well« (Matthew
6:33).

This verse contains the grammar of God for our lives.
When the kingdom of God receives the highest priority
in our lives, then we have the best grammar for the handling of time. When Jesus Himself and His concerns are
our concerns as well, then He will also permit us to suc-
ceed in those areas to which we think we need to give so
much time.

If, however, we write our life according to a different grammar, then from the perspective of God, we have written it
incorrectly. It is like a dictation at school. If the student
does not adhere to the rules of grammar, he will find »fail-
ed« written beneath his work.

That is also how it is with God. It can happen to us, that at
the end we receive a fail-mark for the life we have lived.
»You have been weighed on the scales and found wanting«
(Daniel 5:27). The Bible says: »You will be lost!« In order
that this does not happen, we need the correct »rules of
instruction« for living our lives. Jesus named these for us
in the Sermon on the Mount.

Christians, too, can live according to a wrong grammar.
In Germany, a large percentage of the population would
declare themselves to be Christians. But are they truly

Christians by the Bible's yardstick? In the Sermon on the
Mount Jesus describes such a group of people who consider themselves to be a part of the Kingdom of God, but
who will nonetheless not reach heaven: »Not all who say
to me ›Lord, Lord,‹ will enter the kingdom of heaven, but
only he who does the will of my Father who is in heaven«
(Matthew 7:21). What a tragedy for any who will one day
hear this from the mouth of Jesus!

Membership of a church will not take us to heaven, even
if that church might style itself as the largest, the oldest or
the most wide-spread, but only our actions according to
the will of the Father. We learn the will of the Father
from the Bible. In John 6:28-29, the disciples put this
very question to the Lord Jesus: »What must we do to do
the works God requires?« Jesus answered and said to
them: The work of God is this: to believe in the one [=
Jesus] whom he [= God] has sent.« In the Good News
Bible (1972 German version) this verse says: »What must
we do to fulfil the will of God? Jesus answered: God
requires only one thing of you: you are to trust the One
he has sent.«

This verse refers to a life in which Jesus Christ is our personal Lord. Such a life will always begin with conversion
to Him (see chap. 2.6). Here, in the so-called Christian
West, many believe they are Christians, but they pay little,
if any, attention to God, Jesus Christ and the Bible. They
may not even have heard of a conversion, that is, a conscious and personal turning to the Son of God. Recently,
when I was in conversation with a married couple, the
husband said to me: »We are Christians!« To my question »Do you go to church?« he replied: »No, that doesn't
do anything for me; I would rather go to a concert. That

does more for me.« Sadly, he may even be right in this, because in many churches today, the true biblical Gospel is no longer preached. However, biblically oriented congregations still exist; you just have to seek them out. One can join them and hear the one and only Good News.

If we use the wrong grammar, the wrong syntax of time, we will be eternally lost. We will not reach the eternal goal set by God. A logical order to the flow of events in our lives is also a part of the syntax of time. A farmer does not harvest in winter, nor does one build a house before the plans are drawn up. There is such a thing as an orderly sequence of events in our lives, which is why it says in Ecclesiastes 3:1: »There is a time for everything, and a season for every activity under heaven.« There is a season, too, for the call of God to us. Blithely to ignore it will have dire consequences. Anyone who does not decide misses out on an eternity. The Philippian Jailer, on hearing it, understood in a single night what was involved, and was instantly saved.

An unusual birthday: A man in a village had reached the age of 100. The townspeople wondered how they could appropriately celebrate his birthday. So the Mayor, the leader of the choral society and the representatives of other groups in the village came together to discuss plans for the running of this uncommon celebration. The person celebrating his jubilee was asked what he would like to hear in an oration and what songs should be sung. The old man gave instructions as follows: »You may say and sing anything you want; there are no restrictions whatsoever except this one, which you must adhere to at all costs: I do not want to hear a single word about death.«

Here was someone 100 years old, but who had not gained an ounce of wisdom in all that time. He stands at the threshold of eternity and has planned nothing. 2 Kings 20:1 says: »Set your house in order, for you shall die.« In Psalm 90:12 we are given the following instructive hint: »Teach us to number our days [i.e., to consider that we must die] that we may gain a wise heart.« According to this passage we become wise when we consider that our life is finite, and when we learn to use this perspective to determine what is important and what is incidental in this life.

3. A third biblical rule for the syntax of time: Someone has estimated that in the city of Paris 100 million hours per year are lost through time waiting in traffic jams. Just so, paralyzing »jams« can enter into our lives. They occur through difficulties in the family, in the workplace, in the neighbourhood. Over time, it leads to stress, worry, discouragement and disappointment. Thereby precious time is lost which can never be regained. Here, too, the Bible helps us to an effective management of time: »Let us lay aside every weight« (Hebrews 12:1). By pardoning and forgiving, we rid ourselves of ballast which can mentally bind us, so paralyzing our use of time. We find more important biblical advice in Psalm 1:1: »Happy are those who do not follow the advice of the wicked, or take the path that sinners tread, or sit in the seat of scoffers.« Keeping to the advice of this text will protect us from taking a wrong marriage-partner, or seeking out the company of people who are not good for us. With all His instructions and directives, God desires to protect us from unnecessary heartache and preventable problems, and so to help us to a good syntax of time.

2.5.3 Semantics of time

By semantics of time we mean its thought content. It is indisputable that time, in our lives, has differing qualitative characteristics. We attribute correspondingly different value to time we have lived through, depending on the number of experiences and the pleasantness or otherwise of the things that happen to us. Do we occupy our minds with worthwhile, unimportant, useless or even bad thoughts? Consequently, there is both a positive, as well as a negative semantic ($S > 0$, $S < 0$); $S = 0$ accordingly means there is no thought-content to that time at all.

Football: For a football enthusiast, ninety minutes of spectator-time at the final match of a World Cup Series clearly have a different value from ninety minutes at a match between two unknown village clubs. On 8th July 1990, the final game of the Soccer World Championship between Germany and Argentina took place in Rome, and Germany subsequently became world champions with a score of 1:0. *Andreas Brehme* scored the winning goal in the 85th minute when he converted a penalty. At that time, 73,600 spectators were crowded into the Olympic Stadium. For those present, these were ninety precious minutes. A similar thing happened for thousands of spectators and millions of TV viewers when the final game of the 15th Soccer World Championship was held in Los Angeles on 17th July1994. Brazil won against Italy with a score of 3:2 in a penalty shootout, after a scoreless 120 minutes of play. Beneath the hot Californian sun, 94,714 spectators watched the Final directly. In Germany this World Championship Final emptied the streets – an average TV audience of 17.59 million followed the live transmission on ZDF. The market ratings share was 79 %; never before had a football game without German participation created such great interest in a TV audience.

Time is not equal to time: The entry costs to various functions and performances, and the ratings for TV, are not only objective but also subjective indicators of the differing values we place on our experiences in time. The relative amounts of entrance fees paid (e.g., for Gala Performances, Opening Nights, World Sports Championships) are a measure of how we subjectively rank in value a given event in time. Half an hour at an enjoyable function is experienced differently from half an hour at the bus stop. Equal quantities of time (statistical aspect) can, with respect to content (semantic aspect), be filled up very differently.

Quality of life: It is not the length of our individual time axis (length of life) which makes up our life, but it is, rather, the events (actively shaped or passively experienced) within our lives which determine the quality of life. Jesus Christ came into the world to give our life true semantic quality: »I have come that they may have life, and have it abundantly« (John 10:10).

Positive semantics: The person who is totally secure in God has the best semantics. In Psalm 31:15, the psalmist admits: »My times are in your hand« (This verse addresses several levels at the same time and extends from statistics right through to pragmatics). With God, my time acquires a different, yes a new quality, which extends beyond the purely earthly.

The person who knows himself to be so altogether in God's hand, thereby expresses that he has also sorted out eternal matters. He who has lived his life in such a way that his thoughts and actions were in God's hand will, in death, still go through a deep valley, but he will not be alone. There is One who goes with him; it is the One who said: »I am the Good Shepherd« (John 10:11). Psalm 23:4 says: »And though I walk through the valley of the shadow of death I will fear no evil, for you are with me.«

The Bible wants to help us to good semantics by giving us numerous helpful directives: »Much good comes to a man through the fruit of the mouth, and he is rewarded according to the work of his hands« (Proverbs 12:14). In prayer we can ask God for the plan for our life that is best suited to us and desired by God: »Teach me your way, O Lord, [in this time!], that I may walk in your truth; give me an undivided heart to revere your name« (Psalm 86:11).

To give us as much help as possible, the Bible also mentions people who have no semantics of time, or negative semantics, in order to warn and protect us. Psalm 90:9b says: »We spend our years as a tale [useless chatter] that is told.« What kind of people are spoken of here? On the surface, it would seem obvious that it refers to people who spend their lives aimlessly. Such are definitely included, but more to the point, it speaks of those who only ever want to realize their own selfishly ambitious plans in life. The term self-realization refers to this way of thinking and living.

Zacchaeus was a very active man who was thoroughly dishonest, using his job of tax collecting to cheat people. His thoughts were exclusively focused on temporal issues. No doubt he had invested his money in various expensive villas in Jericho and the surrounding area. Ultimately, he was spending his years uselessly, just like a frivolous conversation, a »tale that is told.« He knew nothing of planning ahead for eternity. Only when he encountered Jesus was there a fundamental change. Now the eternal component was given space in his life. Jesus confirmed this change with the words: »Today salvation has come to this house« (Luke 19:9).

How much precious time we waste on envy. We read about this in Ecclesiastes 4:4 – »Then I saw that all toil and all skill in work come from one person's envy of another. This also is vanity and a chasing after wind.« Many people spend their time doing unimportant things: »They became futile in their thinking, and their senseless minds were darkened« (Romans 1:21).

We humans are often undiscerning and gullible when it comes to the many ideas on offer today (e.g., evolutionism, occult/New Age ideas, and various other philosophical and religious systems). Therefore the Bible rightly warns us: »See to it that no one takes you captive through philosophy and empty deceit, according to human tradition [i.e., the teaching of men].« It is not merely a matter of avoiding the error, but also of arriving at good semantics of time: »Be careful then how you live, not as unwise people but as wise« (Ephesians 5:15).

2.5.4 Pragmatics of time

Pragmatics of time addresses everything we do, all action in time. How can we make the best possible use of time, gain the most from it? Here we can distinguish three kinds of pragmatics P:

$P > 0$ Doing good
  –   Making good use of time

$P = 0$ Doing nothing, zero pragmatics
–   Leaving time unused
$P < 0$ Doing worthless or bad things
–   Wasting time on frivolous activity
–   Spending time in evil activity

Good pragmatics: Everything has its proper time, which is why God intended there to be a time for rest and re-creation beside all our activity: »Six days you shall do your work, and on the seventh day you shall rest« (Exodus 23:12). Our daily work, essential for providing for us and sustaining our lives, belongs to the pragmatics of life as well. If we do this, too, with God, blessing will be attached to it, as numerous Bible passages attest:

2 Chronicles 19:11b – »Deal courageously, and the Lord be with those who do well.«

Proverbs 18:9 – »He who is slack in his work is brother to him who destroys.«

Ecclesiastes 9:7 – »Go your way, eat your bread with joy, and drink your wine with a cheerful heart, for God has already accepted your works.«

Ecclesiastes 9:10 – »Whatever your hand finds to do, do with your might; for there is no work or thought or knowledge or wisdom in the grave, to which you are going.«

Colossians 3:17 – And whatever you do, in word or deed, do everything in the name of the Lord Jesus, giving thanks to God the Father through him.«

Apart from our practical doings, there is also a spiritual component to all our activity. In Acts 17:10 we are told of people who handled the Word of God in exemplary fashion: »Now these (= the believers at Berea) were of more noble character than the Thessalonians, for they received the message with great eagerness and searched the Scriptures every day to see whether these things were so.« Obedience follows upon realization. Jesus tells us in the Sermon on the Mount: »Therefore everyone who hears these words of mine and acts on them will be like a wise man who built his house on a rock« (Matthew 7:24). In the judgment of mankind which Jesus will hold, He judges one group of people with the words: »What you (in your lifetime) *have done* to one of the least of these, my brethren, you have done to me« (Matthew 25:40). These then enter eternal life.

Bad pragmatics: In Proverbs 12:11 we read: »He who follows worthless pursuits is lacking in sense« (German: »He who follows after **unnecessary things** is a fool«). If mention is made here of unnecessary things, it follows that there are necessary things, too. To these could surely be counted all our requirements for life and limb, as well as those of our family. Added to this there are things which make our life pleasant, for which we are thankful and which bring us joy. In the parable of the prodigal son we read: »And they began to celebrate« (Luke 15:24). God shares in our joy when we celebrate, and are happy together.

So what, then, is unnecessary? There are many things that in and of themselves are not at all bad. But if they consume a disproportionate amount of our time and our hearts are tied to them, if they are time-gobblers which hold us back from following Jesus, then they become unnecessary things:

- A hobby that takes up our free time to such an extent, that we find no time for God.
- Friends that hold us back from following Jesus.

- A passion for collecting something, to which we have given our heart.

When He returns, Jesus wants to find us at work in His vineyard. In Matthew 20:6, He admonishes the people to work for God's Kingdom: »Why are you standing here idle all day?« Unutilized time is lost time. Lost time is irretrievably gone; it cannot be collected back from some Lost and Found Office.

Some examples by way of encouragement to positive pragmatics

In the Parable of the Entrusted Talents (Matthew 25:14-30, also the Parable of the Ten Minas, Luke 17:11-27) Jesus advises: »Do business with these until I come back« (Luke 19:13). With these words, Jesus gives us great freedom in our activities. We can all apply our very individual gifts and talents. There is no one, who would not be able to do something. Something will surely occur to us if we make an effort. The following example of an old woman shows how much depends on simply being willing:

A blind African woman: A 70-year-old woman lived in a French-speaking African country. She was blind and illiterate, but she loved God. She owned a French Bible, which she treasured, even though she could not read it. One day she went to the missionary and asked him to mark the text of John 3:16 in red. This he did, without knowing the blind woman's intentions. Then the woman sat with her Bible at the school gate and asked the children as they came out, whether anyone could read French. The children happily admitted to this, for they were proud of their acquired language skills. The woman pointed to the highlighted spot in her Bible and asked if someone could read it to her. This the children gladly did: »For God so loved the world, that he gave his only begotten Son, that whosoever believes in him should not perish, but have eternal life.« The woman then asked, whether they had also understood what they had just read. »No!« was the answer. Whereupon the 70-year-old explained it to the listening students. Through her outreach in this way, 24 men are known to have later become proclaimers of the Gospel.

An entrepreneur: The well-known German evangelist *Wilhelm Pahls* (1936 –) told the story of a Swiss entrepreneur who converted to Christ. Soon after his decision, his mind was firmly made up: I want to serve the Lord with my facilities. He thought of foreign missions and took his concerns to a spiritual counsellor. He prayed with the man for guidance, that he might soon recognize what was right for him.

After some time, the evangelist was back in the same locality. The businessman sought him out anew and reported how God had led him: »Whilst I can run operations well, I cannot preach well. Therefore I decided to use my money to finance people who are going to the missionfield. I began with 10 % of my income, then raised it to 15 % and subsequently to 20 %. My business was more and more successful and so I enlarged my factory. I was also able to raise the percentage of my giving still further. In the meantime I have arrived at 50 % and am able to fully finance 30 missionaries. That is my missions-strategy. Had I gone out myself, I could not have been half as effective.«

With writers in Kirghizstan: I shall never forget that afternoon of 22 April 1993 when, in the company of the interpreter Dr *Harry Tröster* and several other friends, we were travelling as part of an evangelizing tour in Kazakhstan and Kirghizstan. In Bishkek, the capital of Kirghizstan, we received an invitation from a group of writers. About 24 writers had come together, as was their custom at regular intervals. After friendly words of greeting, their President suggested that all participants should introduce themselves and describe their field of activity. One by one they took their turn and each told of his writings. One was a master of lyric poetry and spoke with enthusiasm on the topic. Others told of their works of prose. Then someone related that he had »translated Goethe« into Kirghiz. He described this with great enthusiasm, because he obviously wanted to please us Germans. Over the years, all of them had achieved great things.

Then, after they had gone around the circle, it was my turn. The thought came to me: how can I speak to these people in such a way as to use this opportunity I have been given and share something of the Gospel with them? I was conscious of the fact that most of them came from a Muslim background. So I referred to my own literary activities and told them by way of testimony how I had come to take up writing:

»Actually, nothing was further from my thoughts than writing, as I think back to my time at school. Regrettably, at that time I would rather complete ten mathematical tasks than write just one essay. Not everyone will be able to relate to that, but that's just how it was. So how, then, did I come to write books? A significant event occurred in my life, which caused a dramatic change. In November 1972 I was converted to Jesus Christ after a meeting in the town hall in Brunswick, Germany. I have realized that

He has the best message for us human beings. Never again have the people of the world been told anything as good as has been told them in His Gospel. I saw clearly that we can receive eternal life only through Him. That is why I now write about this message of Jesus. I want to pass on to many people what I have found, which is why I write. I'm pleased that some of my books have been translated into Russian. We've brought these books with us, and each of you will receive, as a visitor's gift, a copy of each title as well as a Bible.« Then I continued:

»What you think and write will be read and learned by the children in the schools and by your countrymen. Through your writings you have a great influence upon your people. I would like to pass on to you some good advice from where I stand: read the Bible, and then write about the thoughts of the Bible, about God and about Jesus Christ. That is the only thing that will remain for all eternity. Everything else is transient. Why, even if we were to write 1,000 books in our lifetime, that would be insignificant for eternity. Let me encourage you to work for eternal values!«

I was surprised at how attentively they all listened. My testimony (including translation) took, I'm sure, more than half an hour. The president thanked me for my contribution, and both he and his fellow writers posed many questions (e.g., What is the difference between Christianity and Islam? Is the Bible true?), to which I was able to respond at length. At the conclusion of the gathering the books and Bibles we had brought with us were made available for distribution. They converged in a body on the literature. Each one now claimed a small stack of books with largely evangelistic content as his own. In this case I am certain that these people will read the books, because they are accustomed to dealing with the written word.

What may the Lord have effected on that afternoon? He alone knows the extent of it, but in the meantime one thing has already become evident. The president who represented them has, in the interim, translated the book »Questions I have always wanted to ask« [G2] into the Kirghiz language. Two years later, when we returned to Kirghizstan, many of the books were available in time for our use.

Some more Bible texts relating to the pragmatics of time

Galatians 6:10 – »So then, whenever we have an opportunity, let us work for the good of everyone, and especially for those of the family of faith.«

Ephesians 5:15,16 – »Be careful then how you live, ... making the most of the time.«

2 Timothy 4:2 – »Proclaim the message; be persistent whether the time is favourable or unfavourable.«

The command of God concerning time

In John 9:4 the Lord Jesus says: »I must do the work of Him Who sent me while it is day; for the night is coming, when no man can work.« Applied to us, that means: »Do the work of the Kingdom of God whilst there are still opportunities; there is a night time coming, and then every possibility is gone.« What kind of night is this?

· In the first instance it is the natural ending of our life in death. Then the day that is given to each one of us will be over. What we have not done by then will remain unfinished.

· Furthermore it is the change in the world situation: We hear from some foreign mission fields that the once-open doors are closing. Then the time of effective working will be over. In our country we still have the opportunity to proclaim the Gospel in all openness and freedom. Let us be thankful for this open door, and use it well.

· In the final sense it is the »night« of the anti-Christian world kingdom. All doors will then be shut. No one will be able to work any more:

- not the most willing
- nor the strongest
- nor the most capable
- nor the most gifted
- NO ONE!

In that night, even those who still want to accept the word of God gladly, will no longer be able to do so. The prophet Amos describes that night as follows:

> »The time is surely coming, says the Lord GOD, when I will send a famine on the land; not a famine of bread or a thirst for water, but of hearing the words of the LORD. They shall wander from sea to sea, and from north to east; they shall run to and fro, seeking the word of the LORD, but they shall not find it« (Amos 8:11-12).

What a terrible night will have fallen! People wanting to believe, but they cannot. If there is anyone amongst us who has not received the Lord Jesus as yet, he should do it today – now is the acceptable time, now is the day of salvation. I do not know whether the Lord will call you again. The Bible says in Job 33:29 – »God indeed does all these things, twice, three times, with mortals.« Then no more. Take hold of salvation today! Just as a missile can miss its target, so our life can also shoot past its goal. We have missed our life if we live it without Jesus.

Be effective in the Kingdom of God in this present time

In Ephesians 5:15-16 we read: »Be careful then how you live, not as unwise people but as wise, making the most of the time.« What does that mean? Consider, with all the wisdom at your disposal, how you can utilize your time in the best possible way and employ it in the work of the Kingdom of God! Time is a »talent« entrusted to you. Each moment is a gift from God and should be managed with care. This is the great privilege we have: We can employ our time for a cause that will outlast all time. *Thomas a Kempis* is the author of a fitting principle for living: »Now, whilst you have time, collect for yourself imperishable treasures.« And another man of God put it this way: »Time is the necessary anteroom or the dressing room for eternity.« If you kill time, you have killed a gift of God's grace.

Television costs time! Let us for a moment compare the time we spend before the television set with the time we spend for the Kingdom of God. How do you think God will evaluate this balance? Someone has penned a »TV psalm« (patterning it on Psalm 23) which points out some of the dangers of this mass medium:

The television set is my god,
I shall not want.
It feeds me with juicy adventures
And leads me to the murky waters of sin.
It poisons my soul,
It leads me on dangerous paths,

For the profit of others.
Yeah, though I may not have anything to do,
I shall fear no boredom,
For you drive it from me,
Your love stories and comedies comfort me.
You prepare many pictures before me –
In the presence of my children –
You befog my head with sensations,
My cup runs over.
Murderers and criminals
Follow me nightly in my dreams,
But I shall abide under the spell of the television for ever.

The American author *Neil Postman* (1931-) wrote the two works of non-fiction »The Disappearance of Childhood« (1983) and »Amusing Ourselves to Death« (1986). In them he raises a protest against the unquestioning surrender to the electronic information society, which leads to the loss of the ability to read and write. According to *Postman* this also leads to the disappearance of the distinction between the world of adults and that of children. He further explains that today's media-society leads to a lack of ties and traditions, and to the endangering of our spiritual existence.

In Hebrews 12:1 we are admonished to »lay aside every weight...[and to] run with perseverance the race that is set before us.« How does an athlete actually run in a race? Does he don a fur overcoat and heavy boots? On the contrary, he lays aside every load that might possibly weigh him down. Let us, too, throw off all those things which needlessly weigh down our time! All time that we spend on worthless things is lost irretrievably from that contingent of time that we could be giving to God. *Ludwig Hof-*

acker once said: »This present time is our time of sowing for eternity. What we sow here, we will reap over there.«

Therefore let us, too, utilize our time in the right way, by planning. It is amazing how, sometimes, especially those people who have no faith basis to their life manage their time most wisely. Take what the Nobel laureate and behavioural scientist *Konrad Lorenz* (1903-1989) said, several years before his death (Brunswick newspaper of March 30, 1980): »All things considered, I now experience an 11th hour panic to such a degree that I no longer attend congresses or go on tours, but solely devote myself to writing.« Here is someone who recognizes that time is short and acts accordingly. We could also take that on board, but with one difference; we are not to suffer any 11th hour panic, because for us it is true what Psalm 31:15 says:

»My times are in your hand«: If our time is in God's hand, then it is always to our advantage. This means three things:

1. Planning our time well. The word to Hezekiah »Bring your house in order« (2 Kings 20:1) doesn't only apply at the time of death, but also on a daily basis.
2. Having spiritual rules by which to act.
3. Heeding what God wants to do with my time.

Time in God's hand ensures that we do not fritter away our years (Psalm 90:90), but invest in God's bank account. That can mean something quite different for each person.

If we live our life in God's time, the number of years no longer matters. An African friend told me of a cemetery in Ghana containing many graves of missionaries from the earliest missionary endeavours in that land. Many lived only a few days in

the country they had wanted to evangelize and then died of
malaria or other tropical diseases. This is told on the tomb-
stones. Now, was all that in vain? Speaking simply from the
human standpoint, we would have to say yes. But these men
went in obedience to the command of God; their time lay in His
hand and was therefore also fruit for eternity. I have often had to
think about the testimony of my Ghanaian friend. He said:

> »One day I was walking across this cemetery and read
> the inscriptions on the tombstones. Something became
> clear to me: What great love from God these men must
> have been filled with, to give up their lives that they
> might bring the good news of salvation to others also.
> The testimony of those tombstones gave me the de-
> cisive impulse to come to Jesus myself.«

So were the lives and the time of these missionaries given
in vain? Absolutely not!

2.5.5 Apobetics of time

With the apobetics of time we address the goal-orienta-
tion in time:

· Do we have a goal-oriented application for the time
  that constitutes our life?
· Do we have the eternal goal in sight?

Goals or intentions?

Two strategies influence our doings: We either have firm
goals before us, or only vague intentions!

1. Intentions: Intentions have no real relationship to time.
They are vague and diffuse, and therefore worthless. We

say »sometime« or »some other time«, and so express our
unwillingness, or our lack of commitment or prepared-
ness. A statement of intention has no time-strategy. If
someone says they would like to climb Mt. Everest sometime, then that is no more than a well-meant intention.
Perhaps they have seen some photos and been inspired
by this mountain range. It would indeed be great to see it
all first-hand sometime, but the sentiment doesn't extend
to a plan in time to carry out the expedition. It does not
go beyond a mere declaration of intention, and is nothing
more than a case of wishful thinking.

2. Goals: Goals, on the other hand, are time related and
therefore effective. If someone says they want to climb
Mt. Everest in the next month, then we may assume that
they have already prepared themselves thoroughly for the
trip. They are in possession of all the necessary maps, the
visa has been applied for, and the required mountaineer-
ing equipment has already been purchased.

The Bible shows us both – people with intentions, and
those with goals. We can readily recognize the different
consequences:

The **Prodigal Son** said: »I will get up [now, at once!!] and
go to my father, and will say to him, ›Father, I have sinned
against heaven and before you‹« (Luke 15:18). That im-
plies that he sets out at once. This was no vague intention. His plan was fixed in time, that is, in the here and
now, without any time delay. He had even given thought
already to what he would say to his father.

The **philosophers of Athens** heard the Gospel of salvation from Paul on the Areopagus. However, most made

no decision, but rather made only a vague declaration of intention: »We will hear you again about this«(Acts 17:32b). It is not known whether they received another opportunity of salvation, because Paul moved on.

The Bible names numerous people who allowed themselves to be guided by their goal and so serve as examples to us with their good apobetics. Here are just two:

Moses: First we will look at a man of the Bible who had an incredible career ahead of him, but who did not take this opportunity. In actual fact, he missed it, because he made a different decision for his life. The Old Testament speaks of him in much detail; he is probably the one person about whom it records the most. In the New Testament we find a very concise summary of his biography. If an entire life is to be recorded in a few sentences, then obviously it will include only the main features. Since this mini-biography is in the Bible, the question arises as to what God sees as most noteworthy. (What would our condensed biography look like?) But note the biography of Moses, found in Hebrews 11:24-26 – »By faith Moses, when he was grown up, refused to be called a son of Pharaoh's daughter ... . He considered abuse suffered for Christ to be greater wealth than the treasures of Egypt, for **he was looking ahead to the reward**.«

As a baby, Moses was hidden from the Egyptians in a woven basket. The daughter of Pharaoh found the little boy among the reeds of the Nile and decided on the spot to bring the baby up as her own. Moses grew up in a privileged environment: He wanted for nothing in Pharaoh's palace. He studied at the best universities of the land, so that it is said of him »Moses was instructed in all the wisdom of the Egyptians and was powerful in his words and deeds«(Acts 7:22). A unique career was assured: he could have become a well-known learned man, or the leader of what was at that time the world's greatest army; or even more, perhaps even Pharaoh of Egypt. I can well imagine that he could have had the largest pyramid in Gizeh built for him, which would have overshadowed the Cheops pyramid in the truest sense of the word. With such a life's path, tourists today would admire the pyramid of Moses as a great attraction, and bring it home on slides. Marketing brochures throughout the world would today invite us to a tour of Egypt using these photos.

None of all this happened! God called this man (Exodus 3) and gave him the task of leading the People of Israel out of Egypt. That meant: first, 40 years of faith-training in the desert, and then to the end of his life another 40 years of wandering in the desert. Can we imagine two more diametrically opposed alternatives in the life path of a person? The secret behind his choice becomes evident if we note the last sentence of his condensed biography: »for he was looking ahead to the reward.« Moses saw beyond what was immediately before his eyes at that moment. He could renounce the throne of Pharaoh and instead spend the rest of his life in the desert. He oriented himself by his goal, he looked ahead to the reward in eternity. He who sees the eternal is no longer attached to the transitory. The Apostle Paul says: »I consider that the sufferings of this present time are not worth comparing with the glory about to be revealed to us«(Romans 8:18). Therefore we want to take a closer look at the subject of eternity in the last section of this book (Part III).

The Apostle Paul: Following his conversion, Paul was a man with definite apobetics for his life: »Forgetting what lies behind and straining forward to what lies ahead, I press

on toward the goal for the prize of the heavenly call of
God in Christ Jesus« (Philippians 3:13-14). With his eyes
firmly on this goal, he was able to cope in every situation:
»I know what it is to have little, and I know what it is to
have plenty. In any and all circumstances I have learned
the secret of being well fed and of going hungry, of having
plenty and of being in need. I can do all things through
him who strengthens me« (Philippians 4:12-13).

Walking with Christ and proclaiming the Gospel are very often fraught with great difficulties and exertions. Even though
the seed may have been sown with tears, the harvest in eternity will be nothing but joyful: »Those who sow in tears reap
with shouts of joy. Those who go out weeping, bearing the
seed for sowing, shall come home with shouts of joy, carry-
ing their sheaves« (Psalm 126:5-6). In his second letter to
the Corinthians Paul describes how he experienced this truth
from the psalm: »As servants of God we have commended
ourselves in every way: through great endurance, in afflic-
tions, hardships, calamities, beatings, imprisonments, riots,
labours, sleepless nights, hunger; ... as unknown, and yet
are well-known; as dying, and see – we are alive; as punish-
ed, and yet not killed; as sorrowful, yet always rejoicing; as
poor, yet making many rich; as having nothing, yet possess-
ing everything« (2 Corinthians 6:4-5, 9-10). Nothing kept
this man from his goal, therefore he could say: »But I do not
count my life of any value to myself, *if only I may finish my
course* and the ministry that I received from the Lord Jesus,
to testify to the good news of God's grace« (Acts 20:24).

Paul is for us a good example of a life that is goal-oriented.
Because he so unequivocally saw heaven as his goal (Philippians 3:13-14), he was able to achieve great things on
earth. He became the greatest missionary of all time. At

the end of his life he looks back, and here again, it is the goal that is decisive: »I have fought the good fight, I have finished the race, I have kept the faith« (2 Timothy 4:7).

Biblical exhortation to good apobetics

Ecclesiastes 11:6 – »In the morning sow your seed, and at evening do not let your hands be idle; for you do not know which will prosper, this or that, or whether both alike will be good.«

1. Corinthians 9:24 – »Do you not know that in a race the runners all compete, but only one receives the prize? Run in such a way that you may win it.«

Colossians 2:18 – »Do not let anyone disqualify you from the prize.«

Colossians 3:23 – »Whatever your task, put yourselves into it, as done for the Lord and not for men.«

Hebrews 2:1 – »Therefore we must pay greater attention to what we have heard, so that we do not drift away [German: »drift past the goal«].«

Biblical warnings against wrong apobetics

Ecclesiastes 5:10 – »Whoever loves money never has money enough; whoever loves wealth is never satisfied with his income.«

Ecclesiastes 11:4 – »Whoever observes the wind will not sow; and whoever regards the clouds will not reap.« (No apobetics!)

Luke 12:20 – »But God said to him, ›You fool! This night your soul will be required of you; and then whose shall those things be which you have prepared?‹«

One can also pass one's time without apobetics: *Nicholas Lenau* (1802-1850) described such people in his poem »The Three Gypsies«, even finding some appeal in this aimlessness:

I came upon **three gypsies** once, lying in a meadow,
As my wagon, in weary agony, crawled over the sandy heath.
The first sat alone, a fiddle in his hands, and in the
evening glow,
Played to himself a fiery little tune.

The second held a pipe in his mouth
and idly watched the smoke;
Content, as though he needed
naught else of this world
For his happiness.

And the third slept at ease, his lute hung in a tree,
And the wind moved softly over its strings,
As a dream moved across his heart.

Upon their clothes these three
wore holes and coloured
patches;
But in themselves defiantly free,
They showed derision for this world's
destinies.

In three ways they showed me, when life looms darkly,
How to spend it; In smoke; in sleep;
and in fiddling,
and so to show it threefold contempt.

Whilst driving on I long loo-
ked back,
To those dark brown faces,
With their black wavy hair.

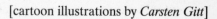

[cartoon illustrations by *Carsten Gitt*]

On the other hand, the following poem advises good apobetics in time (author unknown):

> The time is short, o man – heed wisdom's call,
> This moment well to you avail;
> You make this journey once in all,
> Leave blessing softly in your trail!
>
> Not one hour can you ever hold,
> Before you notice, it has flown;
> Be faithful, wisdom has to you long told,
> A great reward awaits faith's own.
>
> See how fools fritter time away,
> With drinking, joking, resting, food;
> The wise ones work, and win; each day,
> They pass the time in doing good.
>
> Thus, Saviour, teach me now to dedicate
> My years to You in consecrated bond,
> To serve You solely, till I reach death's gate;
> Sowing seeds for that life beyond.

2.5.6 Summary

Chapters 2.5.1 to 2.5.5 above have shown that the intro-
duction of biblical aspects to the phenomenon of **time** ef-
fectively gives it a marked broadening, and also a deeper
explanation. The five-level concept proves to be totally
and equally applicable to time. This will be demonstrated again graphically and by way of summary in the **figures
4, 5** and **6**.

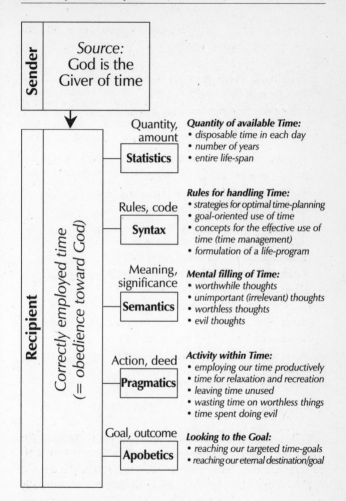

Figure 4: *The five-level concept of time.*
*Man as the recipient of the gift of time from God. Although the meas-
ure/extent of our life-span (statistical aspect) is not in our hand, we
nonetheless have various possibilities of choice open to us on the four
higher levels, due to the freedom given to us.*

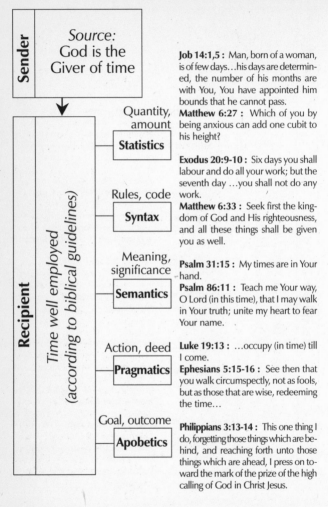

Sender

Source:
God is the
Giver of time

Recipient

*Time well employed
(according to biblical guidelines)*

Quantity,
amount

Statistics

Rules, code

Syntax

Meaning,
significance

Semantics

Action, deed

Pragmatics

Goal, outcome

Apobetics

Job 14:1,5 : Man, born of a woman, is of few days…his days are determined, the number of his months are with You, You have appointed him bounds that he cannot pass.
Matthew 6:27 : Which of you by being anxious can add one cubit to his height?

Exodus 20:9-10 : Six days you shall labour and do all your work; but the seventh day …you shall not do any work.
Matthew 6:33 : Seek first the kingdom of God and His righteousness, and all these things shall be given you as well.

Psalm 31:15 : My times are in Your hand.
Psalm 86:11 : Teach me Your way, O Lord (in this time), that I may walk in Your truth; unite my heart to fear Your name.

Luke 19:13 : …occupy (in time) till I come.
Ephesians 5:15-16 : See then that you walk circumspectly, not as fools, but as those that are wise, redeeming the time…

Philippians 3:13-14 : This one thing I do, forgetting those things which are behind, and reaching forth unto those things which are ahead, I press on toward the mark of the prize of the high calling of God in Christ Jesus.

Figure 5: *The five-level concept of time.*
Time well employed, according to biblical guidelines. On all four levels above that of statistics, we have the freedom to comply with the guidelines of God. If we live according to these, we are being obedient to God.

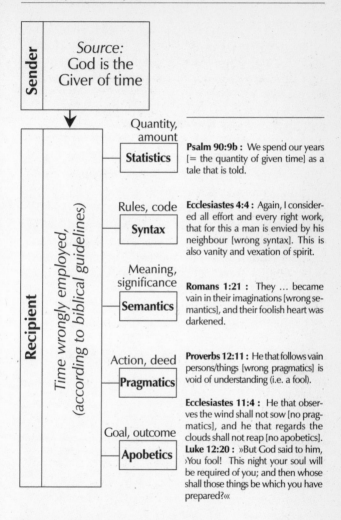

Sender

Source:
God is the
Giver of time

Recipient

*Time wrongly employed,
(according to biblical guidelines)*

Quantity,
amount
Statistics

Psalm 90:9b : We spend our years [= the quantity of given time] as a tale that is told.

Rules, code
Syntax

Ecclesiastes 4:4 : Again, I considered all effort and every right work, that for this a man is envied by his neighbour [wrong syntax]. This is also vanity and vexation of spirit.

Meaning,
significance
Semantics

Romans 1:21 : They ... became vain in their imaginations [wrong semantics], and their foolish heart was darkened.

Action, deed
Pragmatics

Proverbs 12:11 : He that follows vain persons/things [wrong pragmatics] is void of understanding (i.e. a fool).

Goal, outcome
Apobetics

Ecclesiastes 11:4 : He that observes the wind shall not sow [no pragmatics], and he that regards the clouds shall not reap [no apobetics].
Luke 12:20 : »But God said to him, ›You fool! This night your soul will be required of you; and then whose shall those things be which you have prepared?‹«

Figure 6: *The five-level concept of time.*
Time wrongly employed, according to biblical guidelines. On all four levels above that of statistics, we can misuse our freedom and so act contrary to the guidelines of God. Doing this puts us in a state of disobedience toward God.

At the end of chapter 3 we asked whether comparable natural laws could be formulated for time as for information. According to the above detailed presentation, the answer is yes. Therefore we can put two laws of nature[11] on record:

N1: Statistical time is physically measurable.

N2: (Anthropological) time has (in the same manner as information) five hierarchical levels: statistics, syntax, semantics, pragmatics and apobetics.

Several other theorems will also be formulated, but because they cannot be derived from the realm of our experience, they do not rank as natural laws. They are to be found in the Bible, and are therefore also true:

Theorem 1: Time did not always exist. It was brought into existence with the creation of the world.

Theorem 2: Time will not always exist. It has an ending set for it by God.

---

[11] **Laws of Nature:** For further information relating to this topic (What is a law of nature? What criteria need to be fulfilled for a law of nature to be evident? What significance do laws of nature have for science and technology?) see [G1, pp.22-42].

2.6 The most important personal decision in time

Ecclesiastes 3 states: »There is a time for everything«. That applies to God's call to us, also. We don't always get this opportunity for a decision. The heavenly clock does not run according to the atomic clock, but according to the *kairos* of God. God does not call us all of our days. The book of Job states: »God does all these things to a man – two or three times« (Job 33:29). The call of God is meant for you, today. Studying the New Testament, one is struck with the way in which people confronted with the Gospel grasped hold of their salvation on the very same day. Zacchaeus (Luke 19:1-9) was full of curiosity and climbed into a tree, to be able to see Jesus passing by. Jesus approached him, told him what was necessary for his salvation, and he was thoroughly converted. The message of salvation struck the Philippian Jailer (Acts 16:23-34) after midnight. This gentile is obedient to the command, »Believe on the Lord Jesus!« and finds eternal life. Lydia (Acts 16:14-15) hears the saving word while assembling with other women by the river, and finds eternal salvation in Jesus. The thief on the cross (Luke 23:40-43) calls upon Jesus as the Lord of eternity, and is accepted.

If one had asked all of these folk at breakfast whether they wanted to become converted on that day, they would have answered with a clear NO. But God called them in His hour, throwing them the saving lifeline. Note that all of them immediately – on the same day as they heard the news of salvation – grasped hold of it, and with it, eternal life. So too should you heed the call of God seriously as you read these words, and take hold of salvation today. Now could be your hour!

Others were unable (or unwilling) to make the decision.
The rich young ruler (Luke 18:18-23), after his decisive
encounter with Jesus, walked away sorrowfully; his attach-
ment to his wealth ruled out the option of following Christ.
The Athenian philosophers shied away from a decision,
preferring instead to hear Paul again at another time (Acts
17:32). King Agrippa stood at the threshold of conversion when he said, » You almost persuade me to become a
Christian« (Acts 26:28).

The Bible nowhere tells us that these people made a decision for Christ at another time. That is why God gives
us this advice: »Today, if you hear his voice, harden not
your hearts« (Hebrews 4:7). Don't reject His offer today,
lest you miss the eternal goal!

Conversion to Jesus Christ

Over the centuries, people have devised a wide variety of answers to the question, »How do I get to heaven?« The multitude of religions, sects, and »own ways« is testimony to this.

The canoness: A wealthy canoness built a poorhouse providing free board and lodging for 12 women. The only
condition was that they had to pledge themselves to pray,
for one hour each day, for the salvation of her soul. Who
knows whether they actually did this? Perhaps 12 women
are too few – perhaps it really needs to be 24 women,
praying for two hours a day, to obtain entry into heaven?
Who is to set such a benchmark of pure invention?

The man with the spade: After a lecture to business people
at a hotel, I fell into conversation with my neighbour at
the table. I had spoken about Jesus and heaven. Now I
asked this man opposite me whether he believed that he

would go to heaven one day. I was delighted to hear his YES. When I asked him for the basis of his confidence, he replied: »I'm a peaceful man, and I get on well with my neighbours. God sees that, and that's enough.« To this I replied: »It's great that you get on with the people around you, but no one gets into heaven because they do a few good turns and occasionally lend their neighbour a spade.« It is widely believed that, if we do good deeds, this constitutes an entry ticket into heaven. But this is a grave mistake, as we will see.

Are all the different ways of our own devising of any help?
Luke's Gospel contains a remarkable passage about entry into heaven. Someone came to Jesus (Luke 13:23) and asked: »Lord, will only a few be saved?«

Jesus' reply (Luke 13:24-29) emphasizes the gravity of the matter:

> »**Make every effort** to enter through the narrow door, because many, I tell you, will try to enter and will not be able to. Once the owner of the house gets up and closes the door, you will stand outside knocking and pleading, ›Sir, open the door for us.‹ But he will answer, ›I don't know you or where you come from.‹ Then you will say, ›We ate and drank with you, and you taught in our streets.‹ But he will reply, ›I don't know you or where you come from. Away from me, all you evildoers!‹ There will be weeping there, and gnashing of teeth, when you see Abraham, Isaac and Jacob and all the prophets in the kingdom of God, but you yourselves thrown out. People will come from east and west and north and south, and will take their places at the feast in the kingdom of God.«

These sayings of Jesus show us some very important things about people who do or don't reach that final destination, as the case may be:

- Because many people wish to eventually get to heaven, they have devised various ways to get there; one only has to look at all the religions and sects. But in the process, they have not made it easy for themselves. All imagined paths to self-salvation are costly and burdensome; much is demanded of people, and much is imposed upon them.

- All self-devised pathways are strongly condemned by Jesus. The cry of such people, »Open the door for us« is not just left unheard, but is met with a stern rebuff: »I don't know you or where you come from. Away from me, all you evildoers!« They end up in the place of the lost, where there will be weeping and gnashing of teeth.

- On the other hand, there will be many people who reach the kingdom of God. The inhabitants of heaven will have come from all corners of the earth, from every nation, tribe, people and language (Revelation 7:9).

- But how does one get to heaven? This is the most important question that we need to resolve in this life. Next to this, all other questions and problems are trifling and unimportant. Note the challenging exhortation of Jesus, calling us to »make every effort«. In so doing, he tells us that this important matter must be resolved now, at this time, and that it demands action on our part. But this action will be of no use on the other side of death's door, because then all the dice will have fallen. »It is appointed unto men once to die, but after this the judgment« (Hebrews 9:27).

To what, then, has God tied entrance to the heavenly kingdom? On the Mount of Transfiguration God spoke out of the cloud: »This is my beloved Son, in whom I am well pleased; hear him!« (Matthew 17:5) God has presented the Lord Jesus as the object of faith, for our salvation (Romans 3:24-25). Therefore salvation is solely and exclusively tied to the person of Jesus Christ: »He that believes on the Son has everlasting life: and he that believes not the Son [of God] shall not see life; but the wrath of God remains on him.« (John 3:36) Thus could Jesus unequivocally say: »I am the door; whoever enters through me will be saved« (John 10:9). He is the only way to heaven, to the Father's house: »I am the way ... no one comes to the Father except through me« (John 14:6).

Since God has so unmistakably and absolutely tied heaven to the person of Jesus, the following questions take on the utmost urgency: How do we get onto the way of Jesus, how do we go through this door, how do we book heaven for ourselves, each one of us personally? Answer: Through conversion to Jesus Christ! He Himself said: »Unless you repent [Gr. *metanoeo*, be of a changed mind], you too will all perish« (Luke 13:3). In Matthew 18:3 he speaks with equal clarity about this: »Truly I say to you, unless you be converted [Gr. *strepho*, to turn right around], and become as little children, you shall not enter into the kingdom of heaven.« Repentance leading to conversion is thus the absolutely necessary precondition for salvation, which is why this process will now be described in detail in a number of steps (S1 to S7).

S1: Recognizing your condition: Read Romans 3:22b-23 in the New Testament: »For there is no difference here, because all have sinned, and fall short of God's glory.«

This passage shows us our overall lost condition before the living God. Because we have broken all of God's commandments (see the Ten Commandments in Exodus 20:1-17, and the Sermon on the Mount in Matthew 5 to 7) we are sinners before a holy God. Sin separates us from Him, and so we have nothing to commend us to God and make us acceptable to Him. Since the Fall into sin, there is a yawning gulf between the holy God and us sinful humans. We have no access to Him, because He »lives in the light which no man can approach« (1 Timothy 6:16). Are you able to agree with God's diagnosis of your condition?

S2: The only way out: There is **only one way** out of this dilemma, a way provided by God Himself. On the cross, the Son of God was put to death for our sins. Jesus came into the world, to save sinners (Matthew 18:11). Apart from Him, there is no way to be saved (Acts 4:12). Are you able to believe that?

S3: Confessing your sins: We read in 1 John 1:8-9: »If we say we have no sins, we deceive ourselves, and the truth is not in us. But if we confess our sins, he is faithful and just to forgive us our sins, and to cleanse us from all unrighteousness.« On the basis of His redeeming work on Calvary, Jesus has the authority to forgive sins. If we rely on His promise, confess our guilt to Him and ask Him for forgiveness, He is faithful, i.e. we can be completely sure that we will be released from the guilt of sin. But just contemplating this is not enough, we have to actually *do* it! Do you want this? Then tell it to the Lord Jesus now in a prayer (following is some possible content of your freely formulated prayer):

»Lord Jesus, I have heard from You today, and I've understood why You came into this world. In your bottomless love, You have taken hold of me, too. You see **all** my sin and guilt from childhood onwards – not just that which comes to my mind now, but also that of which I am presently unaware, including things long forgotten. But You know everything, every sinful attitude, every false stirring of my heart – everything is recorded with You. I am like an open book before You, and with my life as it is, I cannot stand justified before You. So I ask You now – please forgive all my sin and cleanse me thoroughly. Amen.«

You have now done that which is necessary at the beginning of every conversion, namely asking for forgiveness (1 John 1:8-9). How much of your sin do you think you have now had forgiven? 80 %? 50 %? 10 %? It says here that He cleanses us »from all unrighteousness.« (1 John 1:9) You have had everything forgiven! Yes, everything – the whole lot – 100 % completely! You can *know* this – not just assume it, think it is possible, or hope for it. The Bible regards it as important for us to have absolute certainty in this matter. There are two fundamental passages that give us this surety: 1 Peter 1:18-19: »Know that you were not redeemed with perishable silver or gold…, but with the precious blood of Christ.« The other passage is 1 John 5:13: »These things have I written to you who believe on the name of the Son of God, that you may know that you have eternal life.«

Many are of the opinion that here on Earth we can never know for certain if we will eventually get to heaven. But this view is fundamentally wrong; the above-mentioned passages speak very clearly.

S4: Surrendering your life: The Lord Jesus has forgiven all your sin. Now you can entrust your life to Him. In

John 1:12 we read: »But to all who received Him, to them He gave power to become the children of God, even to those who believe on His name.« All those who invite the Lord Jesus to take over the control of their lives obtain the full rights of a child of God.

We don't become children of God because we have done some good things here and there, or because we are especially pious, or because we belong to some church or another, but because we entrust our lives to the Son of God and are prepared to follow Him in obedience. The far-reaching implications of this step should not be underestimated. It involves the Lord Jesus becoming our Lord and our king. An analogy can illustrate this: Jesus has to become the captain of our life's ship. The captain knows his way around the waters, and where there are dangerous reefs that need to be avoided. That's why he has the authority of command on the ship; he knows the destination , and his orders apply to all. Were we merely to make Jesus an able-bodied seaman, say, on our ship, it would be of no use to us. We ourselves would still be the captain; we don't know the dangers, and we would suffer shipwreck and never reach our destination. Unfortunately, most people sail their life's ship without Captain Jesus, and so they become eternally lost. In conversion, Jesus is made Lord and captain. From now on, I listen to His commands, which we can learn more and more about in daily Bible reading. We now want to affirm this in prayer:

»Lord Jesus, You have forgiven all my sin. I can't even grasp it yet, but I trust Your promise. And now I ask You, please come into my life. Guide me and lead me on the path that You show me. I know that You mean well with me, so I want to entrust every part of my being to You. Help me to lay aside everything which is not right before You. Grant me new habits that come under Your blessing. And give me an obedient heart, that I may do what Your Word tells me to. Let me not give heed to all manner of outside influences and human opinions, but open for me access to the Bible, that I may rightly understand Your Word and live accordingly. Today I'm making You the captain of my life's ship. From now on You are to always be my Lord, and I want to follow after You. Amen.«

S5: Accepted: The Lord has accepted you, for He has promised: »Whoever comes to me, I will not cast out.« (John 6:37) He has paid an immense price for you at the cross (1 Peter 1:18-19), He has rescued you. You have now become God's child. Whoever is a child is also an heir: God's heir, heir to the heavenly realm. Do you have any idea what is taking place right now in heaven? Perhaps you've guessed it – joy! Yes, absolutely! In Luke 15:10 Jesus Himself says: »Likewise I tell you, there will be joy in the presence of God's angels over one sinner who repents.« There is joy in heaven right now over your conversion. The whole of heaven participates in this event, when *one person* takes the message of the Gospel seriously and appropriates it for themselves. When we personally turn to Jesus, the Bible refers to this as becoming converted; in the process, we lay down our sin and guilt and He assumes it. Simultaneously, God works a re-birth in us: He gives us new life as His child, and we receive it.

Conversion, and being born again, thus go hand-in-hand. They are the two sides of one and the same coin.

S6: Thankfulness: Redemption is a gift to us from God. Only through His love has the way of salvation been made possible for us. We cannot contribute in any way to the work of redemption. Anyone who has received a gift says, »Thank you!«. So that's what we want to do now, also. Formulate in your own words a prayer of thanks to God. Tell it now to God, who has now become your heavenly Father, and to the Lord Jesus, your Saviour:

»Dear Father in heaven, You have now become my Father too, and I am able to be Your child. Through Your son, the Lord Jesus, You have freed me from all my sin and guilt and I now have access to You. Lord Jesus, I thank You that you saved me, also, and have given me the gift of eternal life. Amen.«

S7: Where to from here? The Bible compares your current state with that of a newborn infant. Just as a newborn clearly belongs to a family, you now belong to the family of God. Those who are newly born live in a critical phase of life, one in which there is the phenomenon of infant death. This is also possible in the realm of faith. The birth (conversion) has gone well. There is genuine new life. Now nourishment (milk) and good care are absolutely necessary. Naturally, God has made provision here, too, and has done everything in order to enable you to develop and grow well. If we follow God's advice, infant death will be avoided. There are five important points, which are not just important for a life following Jesus: they are **indispensable prerequisites (IPs)** for living with Christ as a practical reality. If we follow **these five IPs** we have God's declared guarantee that we will reach the destination.

IP1: God's Word

You made your decision on the basis of the words of the Bible. The Bible is the only book authorized by God. No other book is anything like its equal, in authority, truth, information content and its origin. For your new life, the reading of this Word is the absolutely necessary nourishment. This aspect is expressed clearly in 1 Peter 2:2: »Desire the pure milk of the word like newborn babies, that you might grow«. The words of the Bible are this milk. Begin reading the Bible daily, to inform yourself about the will of God. It is best to begin with one of the Gospels (e.g. the Gospel of John, or of Luke). Make Bible reading a beloved daily habit. There isn't a day in which you forget to have breakfast or clean your teeth. So be equally consistent here, and augment your daily routine by adding to it this vital point.

IP2: Prayer

Talk daily to your Lord. Through His Word he talks *to us*; He also wants us to talk with *Him*. We do that through prayer. It is a great privilege to be able to tell Him everything. According to the Bible, prayer only knows two addresses: God, who is now your Father, and the Lord Jesus, who is your saviour, your good shepherd, your friend – yes, who is everything to you. The Bible knows of no other »prayer addresses«. Though other people might direct their prayers to other recipients as well, do not do this (any more). Through prayer you will gain much strength, and it will change you in positive ways. All the everyday things – worries and joys, plans and intentions – can be made matters of prayer. Thank the Lord for everything that affects and touches you. Intercede with Him also for the needs of others, and ask that the people round about you might come to living faith. Reading your Bible, and praying, establishes a »spiritual circulation« which is extremely important for a healthy life of faith.

IP3: Obedience

Through reading the Bible, you will find many helpful instructions for all aspects of life, and also for your relationship with God. If you apply all that you understand in practice, you will experience great blessing. It pleases God when we show ourselves to be obedient children, who live according to His Word and keep His commandments. There is no better way to demonstrate our love for our Lord, than to be obedient to Him: »For this is love for God, that we keep his commandments« (1 John 5:3). Where in some instances there are alternative possibilities for action, we generally find in the Bible a binding standard upon which the blessing of God rests. Make it the guideline for your behaviour: »One must obey God rather than men« (Acts 5:29).

IP4: Fellowship

We human beings were meant by our Creator to have fellowship with one another. Seek out and nurture contact with other committed Christians, those who are also aware of the reality of conversion. Only with such are you able to pray and commune together in faith. When a glowing coal is removed from the fire, it rapidly becomes extinguished. Our love for Jesus will cool off, too, if it is not kept alight through fellowship with other believers. So become an active part of a good congregation, an »alive« fellowship where the entire Bible is believed. Such a place is an absolutely indispensable part of our walk of faith; take especial heed of this fourth »IP«.

IP5: Faith

After we have begun in the faith through conversion and

re-birth, we need to grow in the faith and never let go of it again. Paul writes to Timothy: »But as for you, continue in the things which you have learned« (2 Timothy 3:14). At the end of his life, Paul could proclaim: »I have fought the good fight, I have run the race, I have kept the faith« (2 Timothy 4:7). Let us then follow this example, and remain just as faithful.

Conversion is thus not an endpoint, but the starting point of the new life. Now you can also be a co-worker with God (1 Corinthians 3:9). You can play a part in helping other people to experience salvation through Jesus. Conversion has a dual effect – our life on earth now has a new, meaningful, central focus, and simultaneously we receive the gift of becoming God's children, which makes us heirs to eternal life.

Part III: What is eternity?

When we leave the conveyor belt of time, eternity begins for all of us. We humans are eternal creations. Our existence is never extinguished.

Eternity = an infinitely lengthened axis of time? The following picture is occasionally used in an attempt to illustrate the duration of eternity: Imagine the Himalayan mountains as a huge diamond. Diamond is the hardest naturally occurring substance. Once every thousand years, a bird flies to this diamond mountain and whets its beak. By the time the entire mountain range has been worn away in this fashion, only one second of eternity has passed.

As vivid as this picture may be, it is fundamentally false. Eternity is *no* time-span, not even an extremely lengthened one. Otherwise eternity would be like a conveyor belt stretching into infinity. God would be sitting with us on this confining conveyor belt, bound by time just like we are in this life. But this cannot be so, because God cannot be bound by anything. The above-mentioned illustration of eternity is therefore fundamentally flawed.

3.1 Ideas of eternity among various peoples

Various peoples and cultures have contemplated eternity. Here we will only mention a few of their concepts.

a) **The religion of the Egyptians:** In the ancient Egyptian religion, ideas of an after-life, an eternal abode, were particularly pronounced. Pyramids, pharaohs' tombs, and hieroglyphic inscriptions on tombs and obelisks bear clear witness to this.

Mummification: It was believed that being mummified was absolutely necessary in order to enter the hereafter. All people, not just pharaohs and court officials, were mummified after death. The internal organs were placed in a separate vase (canopic). The heart remained in the empty body shell, as the appraisal of the life that had been lived depended on this. It was imagined that in the beyond, the heart would be compared to the weight of a feather. A pure heart was light, and not weighed down by misdeeds, so it was assumed it would be lighter than a feather. If the heart was too heavy, it would be devoured by carnivorous deities, and that was the end of the after-life.

If the death penalty was carried out on someone, death itself was not the worst punishment for them, but the fact that they would not be mummified, and thus miss out on eternity. Mummifiers were, not surprisingly, highly regarded in society. The tradition of mummification came to an end in about AD 300.

Tomb depictions: The passage of an entire life was depicted in tomb drawings. Thus there are pictures about births, seed-time and harvest, hunting, work, festivals and much more. It was believed that the after-life would only contain that which was depicted on Earth. There was also a judgment in the hereafter. The mummy was for the departed's rest. It belonged to the artistic tradition of showing male and female faces only in profile, whereas the shoulders were shown front-on. The reason for these unchanged principles is not known. Servants were also depicted in tombs. (Note: Egyptian society did not have slaves, only servants. These were paid, and had their own possessions.) A servant was glad to be depicted in the tomb of his master. That way his eternal future was taken care of, too. In such tomb drawings one sometimes finds 365 servant figures. This is supposed to mean that in the beyond, they are not required to work every day; rather, each of the 365 servants is only on duty for one day each year.

b) The happy hunting ground of the Amerindians. The quality of life for North American Indians was primarily determined by the success of the hunt. The animals killed provided meat for nutrition and hide for clothing. If one occupied an area with a rich animal population, life's necessities were taken care of. So it is not surprising that eternity was imagined as a place where the hunting grounds never became depleted.

c) The Nirvana of Buddhists. The salvation goal of Buddhists is to attain Nirvana (Sanskrit: Nibbana = to exhale, blow out, extinguish). This involves two aspects:
1. The extinction of earthly existence, bringing to an end a law of causality which leads to a repeated cycle of rebirths on Earth.
2. Attainment of a state of total peace, of absolute, impersonal being.
Nirvana means the complete extinguishing and end of physical existence. A missionary once asked a strict Buddhist Thai lady, »Can you name anyone of whom you can say for certain that, after their death, they will enter Nirvana [i.e., attain the highest destination for a Buddhist]?« Her answer was, »About every thousand years a person is born who, through many rebirths, has laid aside their carnal desires and accumulated so many good works, that they have reached the stage of an ›enlightened one‹. When such a one dies, they attain Nirvana.« This shows clearly how minuscule are a Buddhist's chances of ever reaching the destination for which they strive. How thankful we can be that the Bible presents us with a different surety!

Everyone who has Jesus as Lord can be certain that death is the entry to eternal life. »Whoever hears my word, and believes him who sent me, has eternal life« (John 5:24).

d) The paradise of Muslims: In Islamic teaching, believing Muslims enter paradise after death. This is a realm in which flow rivers of water, honey, milk and wine; it is a place of sensual pleasures, in which Muslims become married to beautiful paradise virgins of unfading charms. It is not hard to recognize in this the projection of the wishful imaginings of this life into the hereafter.

3.2 *The sense of eternity*

In Ecclesiastes 3:11 we read a remarkable passage: »He has made everything beautiful in its time; he has also set eternity in their hearts.« The Creator has given us all a sense of eternity. For this reason, poets and authors who do not come from a position of biblical faith also write about a sense of, and yearning for, eternity that resides within them. The heathen poet *Hermann Löns* (1866-1914) expressed this in the following (freely translated) way:

> I know a land, to which I've never been;
> There flows a river, that is silver-clean,
>
> There blossom flowers, of a perfume pure
> And colours fine with delicate allure ...
>
> A bird sings on this distant shore,
> Its song not heard by me before;
>
> And yet, I know its melody,
> And know of what it sings to me;

It sings life – and death, indeed,
The highest bliss and deepest need,

Time's every joy, eternity's pang,
Of all of this the bird's tune rang;

If I reach this distant foreign land,
The staff of life will flower in my hand;

If not, death was the songbird's sole refrain
Sang me a life of bitter need and pain.

The various religions, and many works of literature, may express the universal yearning for the eternal, but no human being can portray the reality beyond the wall of death. That is reserved exclusively for the living God of the Bible and His Son Jesus Christ. Only Jesus could say: »I am the truth« (John 14:6), which is why we now want to hear Him, in order to obtain certain knowledge about eternity.

3.3 Eternity according to the Bible

A student approached me after a presentation in the city of Mainz, Germany. I noticed her determination to get an answer as she said, »You've just been talking about time and life after death. But what is eternity exactly?« I was surprised to be asked this question by such an attractive young woman. She was so full of life, why didn't she just postpone the question as many other people do? I said to her, »I'm interested to know why this question is so important to you.« She replied, »I was recently diagnosed as having a hereditary heart condition. As it stands, the doctors have given me just a few more years to live. So you see, I **have** to know what eternity is.«

I realized immediately that this was neither a theoretical, nor a quibbling theological question, but a very existential one. I was moved by the clarity and decisiveness with which this young woman was looking for an answer to this fundamental question. Before I could answer her, she told me in no uncertain terms what she didn't want to hear.

She said, »I can imagine what hell is like. I have read *Sartre*, and in one of his pieces he described it quite evocatively: people are locked in a room and cannot understand each other. They can never leave the room. Never. That is hell. I can imagine that. But what is heaven like? That's what I'd like to know.« She continued, »And please don't tell me it'll be singing Hallelujah or praising God unendingly. I can't imagine having to sing forever. Nor do I desire to praise God continually for the rest of eternity. But I know eternity is our goal in life. It has to be something I can look forward to.«

I tried, in my answer, to describe heaven as a place full of joy and love. She interrupted me right away, »That is not precise enough for me. How could I rejoice in a place where there is nothing but joy? One can only feel joy as such when one has experienced its opposite, sadness or anger.«

The young woman challenged me to examine the question more intensively and to answer exactly, according to the Bible. I will never forget that conversation, as it led me to shift the focus of my presentations to the theme of heaven. What a blessing it would be if more people asked such specific questions about life after death!

At the end of our conversation, she said, »Why is so little preached or written about eternity? Why do most sermons only deal with this life? People are being denied something crucial.« She was right, and because of that encounter in Mainz, I have included a chapter in this book which deals with the question of life after death in detail.

The young woman spoke of both heaven and hell. We, too, will deal with both places, as Jesus preached vigorously and repeatedly on both subjects.

3.3.1 What about hell?

During the Vietnam war, a minister went to comfort a dying soldier. The soldier knew he had only minutes left to live, only minutes before he would be faced with eternity. There was only one question burning in his soul: »Minister, is there a hell?« The minister's answer was a clear, »No.« The soldier's reply was equally clear: »If there is no hell, then we don't need you here at all. You should just go home! But, if there really **is** a hell, then you've misled everyone you have spoken to. You're just lying to us here.«

Jesus clearly speaks of hell as a place that exists. His intention is never to scare us, but to warn us and to invite us into the other, equally real place – heaven.

In the Sermon on the Mount, Jesus warns us: »If your right eye causes you to sin, gouge it out and throw it away. It is better for you to lose one part of your body than for your whole body to be thrown into hell. And if your right hand causes you to sin, cut it off and throw it away. It is better for you to lose one part of your body than for your whole body to go into hell« (Matthew 5,29-30).

Let us take yet another passage from the Gospel of

Matthew: »Do not be afraid of those who kill the body but cannot kill the soul. Rather, be afraid of the one who can destroy both soul and body in hell« (Matthew 10:28). Who sends people to hell? It is certainly not the devil, although that might seem likely at first. The devil himself is condemned and will be judged (Revelation12:10; Revelation 20:10). The Judge will make the Last Judgment, and God has set the Lord Jesus to be that Judge. As we read in Matthew 25:41: »Then he [= Jesus] will say to those on his left, ›Depart from me, you who are cursed, into the eternal fire prepared for the devil and his angels‹.«

Towards whom are the warnings about hell directed? Who is being addressed? I always thought that they were directed at the faithless, the outsiders, the thieves and criminals. However, in almost all cases Jesus directs his warnings about hell towards the faithful. He only addresses the Pharisees on occasion, but when he does, Jesus is especially stern with them because of their self-righteousness. They do not receive a *warning,* because hell is *a certain end* for them: »Woe to you, teachers of the law and Pharisees, you hypocrites! You shut the kingdom of heaven in men's faces. You yourselves do not enter, nor will you let those enter who are trying to (Matthew 23:13).«

The British author David Pawson once compiled a list of those deeds which, according to the Bible, lead to hell. This list contains 120 points and names, among others, the following groups of people:

-    the adulterers
-    the homosexuals
-    the debauched
-    the liars

- the miserly
- the proud
- those who follow astrology
- the cowardly
- the slothful
- ...

In the Parable of the Talents, the man who receives one talent says: »Master, ... I knew that you are a hard man, harvesting where you have not sown and gathering where you have not scattered seed. So I was afraid and went out and hid your talent in the ground. See, here is what belongs to you« (Matthew 25:24-25). His Lord answers him, »You wicked, lazy servant! So you knew that I harvest where I have not sown and gather where I have not scattered seed?« (Matthew 25:26). The text ends with the punishment of rejection: »And throw that worthless servant outside, into the darkness, where there will be weeping and gnashing of teeth« (Matthew 25:30). The Bible defines this place of darkness as hell. This servant is neither an atheist, nor a bad person in the usual sense. He is one who knows Jesus. That is why he addresses Jesus as »Master.« Despite this, he is lost. And why? Because he is lazy!

In the Sermon on the Mount, Jesus gives a serious warning to those who habitually have his name on their lips, but will never see the glory of God: »Not everyone who says to me ›Lord, Lord‹ will enter the kingdom of heaven, but only he who does the will of my Father who is in heaven« (Matthew 7:21). The Parable of the Ten Virgins is also about the faithful. But five of them were to find that »the door was shut« (Matthew 25:10). Why? Their way of life reflected more the customs of the time than the

Commandments of God, and Jesus Christ was no longer the centre of their lives. That is why they hear the unexpected words of Jesus: »I tell you the truth, I don´t know you« (Matthew 25:12).

On the third of June 1998, possibly the most tragic railway accident in the history of Germany occurred when a broken wheel caused a high-speed train ICE to derail and slam into a concrete bridge in the small town of Eschede near Hannover. One hundred people died in that accident. On the twenty-first of June, a funeral service for the victims was held in Celle, with the President and the Chancellor of Germany both in attendance, as well as the friends and families of the victims. Of course, in a situation like this, a sermon should offer comfort and support to the relatives. However, the sermon should still be truthful. Both Catholic and Protestant clergy preached that the victims of the accident would all go to heaven. That is not right. We do not know how many of the deceased really knew the Lord Jesus. It would surely be a percentage similar to that among people in our neighbourhood and at our place of work. Unfortunately, there are only few who have truly taken the Lord Jesus into their lives. According to the Bible, only they will be received into heaven (John 3:3).

In a similar situation involving an accident at the time of Jesus, he comments on those on whom the tower of Siloam fell (Luke 13:4). Jesus' answer is worth noting: »But unless you repent, you too will all perish« (Luke 13:5). He uses the event not to bless the dead, but to preach to the living.

One preacher writes: »People used to be afraid of hell. Today, they are afraid of talking about it.« One can only speak of being saved where there is danger to be saved from. Because there is a hell, we need a Saviour. This Saviour is the Lord Jesus: »For God did not send his son into the world to condemn the world, **but to save the world through him** [= Jesus]« (John 3:17). Jesus Himself is the gate to heaven: »I am the gate; whoever enters through me will be saved« (John 10:9).

3.3.2 What do we know about heaven?

The following quip about heaven is from the German poet *Heinrich Heine* (1797 – 1856): »We shall let the angels and sparrows have heaven« (from *Wintermärchen*). Hopefully, he changed his mind after he had written that line, or he is regretting his eternal isolation in the place of darkness.

Heaven as a concept is used in many sayings and forms of speech to describe various aspects of life. When one is happy, one is »in seventh heaven.« Something that is very good is »heavenly.« There is even a delicious flavour of ice cream called »Heavenly Hash.« For most people the only knowledge they have about heaven is what they hear in everyday expressions like that. Is that all that there is to say about heaven?

So what do we know about heaven?

On closer examination it becomes clear that the idioms fall far short of a satisfactory description of heaven. God has revealed a number of specific details about heaven to us. The Bible is the only authoritative source of information — anything else is pure speculation and the product of human imagination. The Bible often addresses this topic, which is the greatest goal given to mankind. Numerous aspects of heaven become clear when we read the

Word of God and apply reason to the understanding of it.
In our study we will occasionally refer to relevant aspects
of our life here on Earth for comparison.

While we can test whether the Bible is right about earthly
things, we have to accept what it says about heaven in faith.
That is why Jesus said, »I have spoken to you of earthly
things and you do not believe; how then will you believe if
I speak of heavenly things?« (John 3:12).

It is almost impossible to grasp that this eternal and almighty God would like to share our company in heaven.
He sends His servants to invite all peoples and nations
until all are in attendance: »Then the master told his servant, ›Go out to the roads and country lanes and make
them come in, so that my house will be full‹« (Luke 14:23).

We have been given an unmistakable description of the
way to heaven so that we don't miss this greatest of opportunities. Jesus states in John 14:6: »No one comes to
the Father except through me«. This word is fulfilled in
heaven. Only those people who have been saved by the
Lord Jesus will reach heaven (John 3:36; 1 John 5:13).

In the ten points which follow we will look at the nature
of heaven in more detail.

H1: *Heaven is the place where we will be perfectly happy*

The French philosopher *Jean Jacques Rousseau* (1712 –
1778) does not get at the heart of the meaning of happiness when he remarks that »happiness is having a healthy
bank account, a good cook and excellent digestion.« *Vol-*

taire (1694 – 1778) states that »total happiness cannot be known, it is not created for man.« This philosopher is also wrong. Jesus can make us really happy. When Jesus talks about being happy, or blessed, it means much more than what we understand by the word »happy« today. The eternal component is important. Jesus saw his main task as saving people (Matthew 18:11). Those who are saved are happy because they are given the glory of heaven. This supreme happiness begins here on Earth and will be perfected in heaven: »Therefore he is able to save completely those who come to God through him« (Hebrews 7:25). Only those who are saved know real joy and happiness.

In heaven, the place without sin, happiness will be perfect and everlasting, for none of the negative aspects of this world will tarnish life there.

Many people must bear unspeakable suffering on this earth. The bookshelves of the world are full of accounts of suffering and innumerable questions as to why an almighty and loving God can allow them to happen.

Ever since the Flood, humanity has not remained immune to catastrophes, large and small. On the first of November 1755, an earthquake in Portugal turned Lisbon into a pile of rubble. Sixty thousand people died. This event did not fit into the view of the world held by most people at the time. Greatly moved and critical, the German poet/author Goethe wrote, »God the Creator and Keeper of Heaven and Earth did not show himself to be fatherly in his punishment of both the righteous and unrighteous.«

There is no shortage of accounts of terrible suffering. The

high number of victims does not matter, whether six million or sixty thousand. The death of even one person is enough for us to ask: »How could God allow this to happen?« In the life after death, all traces of suffering will be erased. There, nothing will remind us of pain, war, hate or death. »He will wipe every tear from their eyes. There will be no more death or mourning or crying or pain, for the old order of things has passed away« (Revelation 21:4).

Our body will then be freed from all disease and frailty. It will never have to fight with germs, viruses, infections, diseases of the heart or lungs. There will be no such things as hospitals or prisons. There will be no more need for doctors, nurses, police officers, prison wardens or gravediggers.

Once we are in heaven, nobody will want to return to Earth. The time of burdens and worries will be over forever.

The Prussian king *Frederick the Great* (1712 – 1786) named his castle in the city of Potsdam near Berlin *Sanssoussi* (without worries) but led a life full of worries. *Sanssoussi* would only be a correct description of heaven. Heaven is the only place where there is no fighting, no war, no hate, no unfaithfulness, no worries and no broken hearts.

H2: Heaven is the place of everlasting celebration

How do we prepare for a celebration? The yearly presentation of Oscars took place in Los Angeles on March 23 1998. It was a gala party of film, to which previous Oscarwinners, sponsors and many actors were invited. One magazine described the Oscar time-stress as follows:

>Pre-Oscar:
three months to go: book appointment with hairdresser
one month to go: visit spa
10 days to go: get hair cut
3 days to go: visit tanning salon

On Oscar Day:
morning: work out, shower, wash hair, eat light meal
lunch: wait for hair stylist
afternoon: wait for make-up artist
4pm exactly: guests must be in auditorium

Then the doors close. The dice have been cast. ›And the Oscar goes to…‹ «

As this example shows, the preparation for a celebration which only lasts a few hours can take tremendous effort. Most of the effort is spent on beauty. In this world, everything deteriorates, and beauty fades. The effort to compensate with artificial means increases with age. None of this will be necessary in heaven. There we will all be beautiful. More precisely: we will all be *glorious*, and glorious is the superlative of beautiful.

Jesus is described even in the Old Testament when we read, »The Lord reigns, he is robed in majesty« (Psalm 93:1). He is the »glorious Lord Jesus« (James 2:1). On His return, He will come in all His power and glory (Matthew 24:30). In John 17:22, He prays to His Father: »I have given them the glory that you gave me.«

God has a problem: How can He make us humans understand the glory and festivity of heaven? Jesus explains in a parable: »The kingdom of heaven is like a king who

prepared a wedding banquet for his son« (Matthew 22:2).
A wedding is the most beautiful celebration on earth.
Everything is prepared, down to the last detail:

- beloved guests are invited
- the best food and finest drink will be served
- no problems will be discussed on the special day
- the bride will look more beautiful than ever before, and
  will wear the most beautiful and most precious dress of
  her life
- everyone will have a good time

In using this well-known picture, Jesus tries to describe
heaven to us as an unusually beautiful celebration. At
the Last Supper, He says to His disciples: »I tell you, I
will not drink of this fruit of the vine from now on until
that day when I drink it anew with you in my Father's kingdom« (Matthew 26:29). That wine will be like nothing we
have ever tasted here on earth. I also believe we will eat
in heaven. How else are we to interpret Luke 12:37: »He
[= Jesus] will dress himself to serve, will have them re-
cline at the table and will come and wait on them.«

We can safely assume that it will be a richly set table. The
earthly concepts of »costly« and »precious« are too weak
to describe what we will find in heaven. But it is clear
that heaven is festive.

Now comes the surprise: Heaven is not just comparable to a
wedding, but is the place where a real wedding occurs. In
Revelation 19:7 we read, »Let us rejoice and be glad and give
him glory! For the wedding of the Lamb has come, and his
bride has made herself ready.« Jesus Himself is the groom,
and all who have been saved through Him are the bride.

Those who are invited can consider themselves happy. In the Parable of the Lost Son, we read that »they began to celebrate« (Luke 15:24). Joy is everlasting in heaven; we cannot estimate the degree of this happiness.

H3: Heaven is a beautiful place

Jesus said in the Sermon on the Mount, concerning this Creation, »See how the lilies of the field grow. They do not labor or spin. Yet I tell you that not even Solomon in all his splendor was dressed like one of these« (Matthew 6:28-29). The creation displays the Creator's love of beauty, which mankind cannot imitate. God is the originator of all that is beautiful.

After much suffering, God blessed Job: »And he also had seven sons and three daughters. The first daughter he named Jemimah [= little dove], the second Keziah [= cinnamon blossom] and the third Keren-Happuch [= precious vessel]« (Job 42:13-15). The beauty of Job's daughters is especially emphasized. They would have won any Miss World Competition.

Of Jesus Himself, the Creator in person, it is said in Psalm 45:2: »You are the most excellent of men and your lips have been anointed with grace, since God has blessed you for ever.« When He is sacrificed on the cross for the sin of humanity, however, He gives up His beauty, as we can read in Isaiah 53:2, »He had no beauty or majesty to attract us to him, nothing in his appearance that we should desire him«.

Jesus has always been described as beautiful and perfect. In Isaiah 33:17 it is written: »Your eyes will see the king in his beauty.« The well-known German song *Fairest Lord Jesus* expresses this aspect especially well:

Fairest Lord Jesus, Ruler of all nature
O Thou of God and man the Son
Thee will I cherish
Thee will I honour
Thou my soul's glory, joy and crown.

Fair are the meadows, fairer still the woodlands
Robed in the blooming garb of spring
Jesus is fairer
Jesus is purer
Who makes the troubled heart to sing.

Fair is the sunshine, fairer still the moonlight
And fair the twinkling, starry host
Jesus shines brighter
Jesus shines purer
Than all the angels Heav'n can boast.

...

Beautiful Saviour! Lord of the nations!
Son of God and son of man!
Glory and honour,
Praise, adoration
Now and forevermore be thine.

(From the German »Schönster Herr Jesus«, 1677)

If God's love for beauty is evident even in this Creation, in the form of every snowflake, each lily, orchid and the countless blooms of other flowers or the luxurious plumage of some birds, how much more fitting it is to have beauty as one of the most important attributes of heaven!

Many people seek beauty on this earth. Surgeons who perform facelifts are in great demand. An entire industry specializing in the making and selling of beauty-enhancing or beauty-preserving products is assured of thriving business. Yet, even the most renowned of this world's Beauty Queens will see their beauty fade. Everything on earth is perishable (Romans 8:20).

The Empress *Elisabeth of Austria*, better known by her nickname *Sissi* (1837 – 1898) was known in the 19th century as the most beautiful woman in Europe. She was so vain that she would not have her portrait painted after her thirtieth birthday, let alone have photographs taken of her. The German author *Annelie Fried* writes, »Female television hosts reach their use-by date at the age of forty. After that, the nation watching from their living rooms counts the wrinkles.«

Heaven, in contrast, is a place of everlasting beauty. All who have gone there will stay beautiful forever. When we become like Jesus (1 John 3:2), we will also receive His beauty. The earthly value of looking »forever young« is not nearly adequate to describe the heavenly ideal.

H4: Heaven is where our lives will be fulfilled

Most of mankind live below the poverty line. Forty thousand children die daily because they do not have enough to eat. Others are rich; they can afford whatever worldly goods their heart desires and yet are unhappy. Many suffer from depression and worries, or are simply bored.

Jesus is aware of both emotional and physical human needs. »When he saw the crowds, he had compassion on them, because they were harassed and helpless, like sheep without a shepherd« (Matthew 9:36). He wants to help especially here; that is why in John 10:10 He gives as the main reason of His Coming: »I have come that they may have life, and have it to the full.«

Converting to Jesus changes our lives so fundamentally here on Earth that we can clearly see the difference between the old and the new life (Romans 6:4; Colossians 2:6; 1 Peter 4:3). However, it is once we are in heaven that our lives become completely fulfilled. There, we will know for the first time what true quality of life means.

A critic once said that he would never feel like sitting on a cloud and playing a harp for ten thousand years. That is a fabricated picture of life after death, one which we do not find in the Bible.

Heaven is life in abundance. The concept of scarcity is not known in heaven. There is nothing there in need of improvement. Boredom is also unknown, for heaven is complete and offers a life of fulfillment.

While hell can be described as a place of lasting unfulfilled desires, there will be no more yearning in heaven. This does not necessarily mean that all our earthly desires will find their fulfillment in heaven, but that the richness of heaven will be shared with us — a richness which we cannot even imagine — a richness which will make earthly desires superfluous.

When we experience beautiful moments here on earth,

we want to hold on to them. That is what *Goethe* describes when he writes, »Stay but, thou art so fair!« Cameras and videos capture the past; they do not represent life. Heaven, on the other hand, could be described as *everlasting simultaneousness*. Nothing is constrained by mortality. Everything is permanent.

Here on Earth, we can only be in one place at one time. Each move brings separation from people we love. Saying »good-bye« is often painful. In heaven, we will never have to say »good-bye.«

H5: Heaven is a home for us

The architects of this world continually invent new types of buildings. *Jörn Utzon*, the architect of the Opera House in Sydney, Australia, used a peeled orange as his inspiration. We admire powerful palaces of glass and soaring towers of concrete. An architect once wrote that »architecture unites the demands of art with technical perfection. Architecture has been the expression of humanity's yearning for the eternal. Besides architectural works of genius, monuments such as the Great Wall of China and the Pyramids of Gizeh count as some of the longest-lasting works of human hands.«

In a nineteenth-century spa resort on the North Sea island of Juist, a special building was reopened in 1998 after massive reconstruction. The *White Castle by the Sea*, as it is called, located on a high dune, is the first sight on approaching the island by water. Besides the five-star hotel complete with ballroom, restaurant, children's play area and exclusive bar, private apartments are also available in the hotel at the astronomical price of approximately $US 50,000 for 80 m² (= 861 square feet). However, even the most luxurious apartments cannot offer both a sea view and bright sunlight. The apartments facing north have the sea view, but have no direct sunlight. If you want a sunny apartment you have to do without the sea view. Even in this amazingly beautiful and expensive place you can't have everything.

After we die we will live in a home that was designed by Jesus. What the Creator of the world can build is something that no earthly architect could even dream of. Jesus says, in John 14:2-3, »In my Father's house are many rooms; if it were not so, I would have told you. And if I go and prepare a place for you, I will come back and take you to be with me that you also may be where I am.«

Jesus has been building our home for over two thousand years. How beautiful must therefore be the result! Any earthly comforts provided in the spa resort of Juist will be superseded by our home in heaven. If, in this Creation, even every snowflake and each acorn leaf is unique, then how much more will this be true of homes built by Jesus! There is no repetition; everything is especially tailored for the person who will reside there. We have a place in heaven for ever, under a sun that never sets.

H6: *Heaven is a place where we shall reign*

Heaven will be a place of singing and rejoicing for us, but we will also have duties: »And they will reign for ever and ever« (Revelation 22:5).

In the Parable of the Ten Minas, described in Luke 19:11-27, each servant receives ten minas and is told to put this money to work. One servant increases the amount by ten, another by five. When Jesus judges, the first servant is told, »Well done, my good servant! ... Because you have been trustworthy in a very small matter, take charge of ten cities« (Luke 19:17). The second servant receives, in turn, what he deserves, »You take charge of five cities« (Luke 19:19).

We may conclude that, after we die, the responsibility of reigning will be handed over to us. The assigned areas will not be equal in size, but will depend on how hard we have worked for God's Kingdom here on earth. In heaven, we will reign together with Jesus. We have a part in the ruling in eternity.

Here, politicians do everything and anything to get elected. The position of governing will be handed to us in heaven. This task will involve many creative and changing duties. Completing our duties will be easy, for there will be no job stress, no ladder to climb, and no politics in heaven.

H7: Heaven is the place where Jesus is

Sometimes, historical meetings have wide-reaching consequences. For example, we owe the knowledge of how to make porcelain to the meeting of the physicist *Ehrenfried Walter v. Tschirnhaus* (1651 – 1708) and the alchemist *Johann Friedrich Böttger* (1682 – 1719). Even today, something special can grow out of a surprise meeting, especially if God's hand is behind it. Two people who have never before met are brought together. They develop a common understanding about something and act accordingly, with significant consequences.

The one single meeting that has the most significant and wide-reaching consequences is when a person meets with God. That person then finds everlasting life in Jesus. The Bible mentions many such meetings. Zacchaeus, the corrupt chief tax collector of Jericho, changed his way of life and became a believer (Luke 19:1-10). The finance officer of Ethiopia was looking for God in Jerusalem and found Him in the desert. Only after becoming secure in the knowledge of his salvation, does he go on his way, rejoicing (Acts 8:26-39). Saul became Paul through Jesus. Once a persecutor of Christians, Paul became the most important missionary of all time (Acts 26:12-18). In the same way, everyone can meet Jesus uniquely, if we approach Him with openness. Those who dare to meet Him are rewarded with entry into heaven.

Jesus prays to His Father in John 17:24, »Father, I want those you have given me to be with me where I am.« This prayer is fulfilled in heaven. We will be with Him for all eternity. When faith is fully revealed it will be replaced by wonder. When the Queen of Sheba arrived at the court of Solomon she cried in surprise, »Indeed, not even half… was told me« (2 Chronicles 9:6). This expression of surprise will be even more fitting when we arrive in God's kingdom. Here, on earth, there are still many pressing questions, to which we seek answers. There, with Jesus, everything will be explained: »In that day you will no longer ask me anything« (John 16:23).

»There will be no more night« in the presence of God and Jesus (Revelation 22:5). We will no longer need sleep, therefore we will not need beds in heaven. The sun will shine forever. Yet it is not a celestial body which will provide the light. No created sun will shine for eternity, but »the glory

of God gives it light, and the Lamb is its lamp [= Jesus]«
(Revelation 21:23). Isaiah saw the everlasting sun propheti-
cally in God's kingdom: »The sun will no more be your light
by day, nor will the brightness of the moon shine on you, for
the LORD will be your everlasting light, and your God will be
your glory. Your sun will never set again« (Isaiah 60:19-20).

Thousands of people flock to overflowing beaches in their
holidays to soak in the glowing sun. Most of them get nothing more than sunburn and have to live with the danger of
skin cancer, worrying whether or not the SPF of their sun-
block lotions is high enough to screen out harmful rays.
However the everlasting sun of heaven will be good for us
and will never burn. It will not be the scorching sun we
know in the deserts of this earth (Revelation 7:16).

H8: *Heaven is a place without sin*

Shortly after a lecture, a visibly agitated young man approached me, clutching a note. He had made a list of
questions on five matters which he urgently wanted answered. I will never forget his batch of questions on one of
the issues which went straight to the core of the Gospel:

»If God is all-powerful, and is a God of Love, why doesn't
He just let all people into His Heaven? Why did His Son
first have to die on the Cross in order to give us access to
Heaven? Why did God go about this in such an incredib-
ly involved way? Wasn't there a simpler way? After all,
only a small minority will take up the offer of eternal life.«

I was fascinated by this challenging question; here was
someone who wanted to be able to understand and re-
flect somewhat about the way to Heaven, not just blindly

believe. Thinking through it, I myself came to a plausible
answer, too. On the night, I explained it to him as follows
(even though my answer was not as extensive as here, he
could assent to it, and through the insight gained, he was
converted to Jesus that same day): Looking at the history
of mankind, it can fairly be described as a virtually endless succession of wars. The fratricide by Cain was the
beginning of an unstoppable escalation of murder. In all
centuries, ghastly wars have been fought, and people put
to death in all conceivable ways. The Crusades left a wide
trail of blood in their wake. The conquest of South America saw entire peoples eradicated in the lust for power
and riches. In the 1572 Massacre of St Bartholomew's
Day, Queen Catherine used the presence of numerous
Huguenots, at her daughter Margaret's Paris wedding to
Henry of Navarra, to bestially slaughter them. Between
2,000 and 3,000 Huguenots were murdered in Paris — in
the provinces, a further 12,000 to 20,000 people.

The march of technology has permitted more »effective«
killing machinery. In the 20th century we have experienced
the most gruesome escalation of slaughter. In two World
Wars, hate was preached among the nations, and in the
end the score was: countless millions of dead, unspeakable suffering and devastated cities and countryside. Many
countries were forced into communism. The 1998 »Black
Book of Communism« gave the total number of victims
sacrificed to this ideology as 80 million. Nazi ideology
developed a hitherto-unheard-of strategy of elimination,
aimed particularly at the Jewish people. In the death
camps of Auschwitz and Treblinka, among others, six million people were systematically poisoned in gas chambers
and subsequently incinerated. That is about the same as
the entire 1998 population of the state of Israel.

Is it only wars that bring suffering and want? In Germany up to a while ago, every third marriage ended in divorce. The trend today is heading towards every second one ending in front of a divorce court magistrate. The figures may be a little different in other countries, but not markedly so, and the trend is in the same direction. Imagine the pain involved for the partners, and especially for the children involved! Often the divorce is preceded by a long period of fighting, insults and abuse.

We only have to look in any newspaper to read, every day, of corruption, betrayal, child abuse, murder and violence. Criminal offences pad out the lines of the tabloids. Lying and deception, marital unfaithfulness and sexual crime are daily fare.

The German newsmagazine *Der Spiegel* (no. 13 of 23/3/98, p. 234) described the escalation of evil at the end of the second millennium as follows: »We find ourselves at the end of an unfathomable century, one whose technical achievements, whose wars and catastrophes have not only opened our eyes, they have forced us to see – no, more than that – this century literally cut off our eyelids, mercilessly, so that we have been left with no possible way to shield ourselves from having to acknowledge the capacity of human beings for evil and atrocity.«

If we wanted to summarize all this, one short sentence gets right to the point: We live in a world which is permeated by sin.

But what is the cause of all these sins, whose number and variety is immense? It all began with **one single** sin in the Garden of Eden. God had given man everything he needed. There was not even the slightest shortage. Despite this, man decided on disobedience towards God. From then on, the calamity took its relentless course. At the beginning there were not a thousand or a hundred sins. The inferno of all the misery and agony in this world was set off by the spark of just one sin. Just as the law of gravity describes the relentless tendency of all things to keep falling, so too does sin have its own inexorable »law of gravity«: one sin gives birth to the next. It is not possible to exaggerate the harmful nature of sin. Its destructive power has a strongly escalating, even exponentially intensifying effect.

The Bible states a relationship as inevitable and unerring as any scientific law: »The wages of sin is death« (Romans 6:23). This has a dual meaning; sin brings forth not only bodily (biological) death, but a much more awful eternal death. This eternal death, also known as the second death (Revelation 20:6) means not just the extinguishing of our existence, but the continuation of existence in absolute removal from God. All the negative aspects of this world with its suffering and pain, sickness and death are thus in no way some sort of »given« conditions, »the way things just are«. They only came into this world as a consequence of sin. It bears emphasizing once more: **one single, solitary sin is the cause of all the horror and ugliness in the world today.**

I asked the young man: »What would happen if God were to let us into Heaven just as we are?« He immediately replied: »Then Heaven would be ruined!« Yes, that's the way it is; were God to let just one single sin into His Heaven, then soon everything there would look like here on Earth. Following the »gravity law« of sin, its relentless destructive effects would also corrupt the wonderful Heaven of God. In this place of peace, joy and love, suddenly death, sickness and hate would gain entry, and Heaven would no longer be Heaven. But God does not want that under any circumstances! That is why He takes sin so seriously and blocks its every access: »Nothing impure will ever enter it« (Revelation 21:27). Out of love for those who are within, He can absolutely never, in no way, allow even one sin access.

In this world, there is no action that can be undertaken to remove sin. Not even the greatest religious effort would be enough to set aside a single sin. Ever so many good deeds would still not be able to compensate for sin. So the only place mankind would have left to it would be the place of utter remoteness from God. But this place is a place of unforgiven sin. Because sin reigns there, it is a place of lostness and damnation. The Bible refers to it as Hell.

But in His merciful love for us, God has done something against sin which no person would ever have thought of. There is only one solution that can dissolve sin, and that is the blood of Jesus. So the Son of God had to come to this Earth and live here for a time. After which He had to die on a cross, completely innocent and guiltless. That was the only possible way to erase the sin and guilt of mankind. This bitter price for sin was paid by God Himself in the person of His Son. God actually censures man about the enormity of the undertaking made necessary by our sin: »You have burdened me with your sins and wearied me with your misdeeds (Isaiah 43:24).«

In Revelation 22:3, the Bible describes a condition which for us is barely imaginable, namely the sinlessness of Heaven: »There shall be no more curse.« Because of its destructive effects, God abhors sin utterly. But God loves man so much, that He wishes to have eternal fellowship with us. However, for the reasons already covered, He cannot possibly let us into Heaven with our sin. A sinful person and Heaven are two mutually exclusive things. Jesus expressed this concept in a parable in Matthew 22:11-13. That is why the man without a wedding garment — a pictorial representation of purity — was not only removed from Heaven, but irrevocably cast into the outer darkness. In Heaven, no sin or impurity will be tolerated. That's why we can look forward to Heaven. Because it is a place that is absolutely free of all sin, there is no pain or suffering there. Love and joy are its defining characteristics.

H9: Heaven is a place of welcome and enjoyment

Revelation 2:17 contains a remarkable passage about Heaven, although this word doesn't even feature in it:

»To him that overcomes, I will give to eat of the hidden manna, and will give him a white stone, and in the stone a new name will be written, known to no one else.«

The verse introduces three concepts which were known in antiquity but are largely obscure today:

– the hidden manna
– the white stone
– the new name

1. The hidden manna: This refers to something edible.

This concept surfaced already during the 40-year desert wandering of the nation of Israel, when God provided manna for the people to eat (Exodus 16:35). It was a mysterious foodstuff, which was only available until the people had reached the Promised Land. The above verse from Revelation affords us a glimpse into Heaven. The hidden manna is the food of eternity; it is a heavenly foodstuff which is incomparable to anything earthly. This makes it plain that there will be eating in Heaven. Granted, it won't be fillet steak with roast potatoes, Lobster Thermidor, or Black Forest cherry cake. Instead, it will be a food, as yet completely unknown to us, with an incomparably wonderful taste that we cannot even begin to imagine.

Those to whom the thought of relishing food and drink in Heaven is new are referred to two further sayings of Jesus in this regard. In Matthew 26:29 Jesus is teaching the disciples during the Last Supper: »But I say unto you, I will not drink henceforth of this fruit of the vine, until that day when I drink it new with you in my Father's kingdom.« The wine at the wedding in Cana was already superb, but not even the best earthly vintage will be able to compare in goodness and quality with this heavenly wine. Because everything in Heaven is perfect, that includes the heavenly wine — it can be richly savoured with no fear of intoxication, its enjoyment accompanied by neither drunkenness nor hangover.

Luke 12:37 speaks of Jesus the heavenly host: »He will dress himself to serve, will beckon them to the table and will come and wait on them.« What is written here is almost inconceivable for us: we would expect that the Lord of all lords, the King of all kings, would let Himself be waited upon by His people, just as the powerful of this

world might do. Here it is precisely the other way around;
Jesus Himself will be serving heavenly delicacies and heavenly wine.

At the heavenly feast table the motto »enjoyment without
regret« applies in full. Everything is abundantly at hand.
No-one need hold back, because here there is no more
need for diets. Nobody need be concerned about figure-
destroying pounds, or about high blood pressure or cho-
lesterol. All of that belongs to the remote past now, because all things have become new. Nothing will be allowed to diminish the enjoyment, because God wants the joy
to be total and complete.

Regarding **eyes** and **ears**, 1 Corinthians 2:9 says, »Eye
has not seen, nor ear heard, neither has any mind conceived of the things which God has prepared for them
that love him.« In Heaven our ears will encounter something which has no earthly comparison: no choir of this
world, no piece of music, no symphony nor opera can
remotely approach its quality. The same will therefore
apply to our **taste**: that which no tongue or palate has
ever sampled, and no connoisseur of this world has ever
eaten, has been prepared by God for us. God satisfies
all conceivable hunger, even the hunger for a fulfilled
life.

2. The white stone: The white stone, or the white marble
tablet, was a commonly occurring theme in olden times.
Three usages are known from antiquity:

a) Legal proceedings: After a trial, the accused was handed
a stone. A black stone signified a guilty verdict, a white stone
meant acquittal. With this picture, the exalted and resur-

rected Lord describes an aspect of Heaven. At the Cross, Jesus won for us the white stone. Those who receive it are guaranteed acquittal in God's courtroom (John 5:24). No more will we be accused on the basis of our sin. That applies for all eternity.

b) Sport: In antiquity, the highest honours went to that sportsman who emerged as the ultimate victor of a competition. For his outstanding achievement, he was rewarded with a white tablet. This gave him the lifelong right of free entry to all public events like theatre performances or sporting competitions. With this picture, Jesus expresses our free access to Heaven.

c) Hospitality: In antiquity, a host would hand his guest a white stone as a gesture of especial welcome. This custom is used in Revelation to make it clear to us that Jesus regards us as very welcome in Heaven!

We humans pay a lot of money just to be able to see or hear something special.

- Outrageous prices are paid to be at the opening ceremonies of the Olympics, for example. At the 1996 Summer Games in Atlanta, tickets cost over one thousand dollars each, not to mention the even more inflated prices of the ticket scalpers.
- The concerts of famous conductors are popular among those who wish to treat their ears to something special. The first-night performances of plays are just as sought-after.
- For tennis or football fans, the finals in Wimbledon or the Superbowl game are a special treat.

All that we now consider attractive, beautiful to look at, or a pleasure to hear, pales in comparison to heaven. The Bible describes both the wisdom of God as well as heaven fittingly when it says: »No eye has seen, no ear has heard, no mind has conceived what God has prepared for those who love him« (1 Corinthians 2:9).

Not just our eyes and ears but all our senses will be satisfied in heaven. That includes, for example, our tastebuds but also much, much more — everything that makes us feel good will be available in heaven: love, peace, joy, friendliness, goodness.

H10: In Heaven we receive a new name

In the previous chapter H9 we had a closer look at Revelation 2 verse 17. Now we want to focus on a special phrase of great significance within the verse:

»In the stone a new name is written«

When someone we haven't seen for a long time recognizes us again, and addresses us by our name, we sometimes feel pleasantly surprised, even honoured by this. Being called by one's name is something very personal and individual. It feels good, too, when someone tells us that they value us. Doesn't that say something about humanity in general? Obviously, we are attuned to recognition, being made to feel significant, respected and esteemed. Just looking at the various structures in our society — clubs, unions, the military, government and so on — one quickly gets the impression that the hunger for esteem and recognition can never be satisfied in this world. We express that in a number of ways:

Through awards and distinctions in all manner of organizations.
Through decorations for bravery in the military, such as e.g. the British Victoria Cross, the US Congressional Medal of Honor, and the German Knight's Cross.
Through prizes in the fields of science and literature.
Through various degrees and titles.

The desire for esteem and honour is so great, that we even have such titles as:

Honorary citizen
Honorary doctor
Honorary president
Honorary chairperson

People are honoured in a variety of ways, and in the most different of areas:

Sport: Many sportspeople go through years of hard training, so they can, just once, stand upon the victor's podium at the Olympics, for only a few minutes, and receive a medal. In the year 2000, in the city of Rotenburg-on-Fulda (Germany), the *International Federation of Football History & Statistics* chose the world's soccer player of the century. The Brazilian *Pele*, with 1705 points, won this distinction.

In *science* the pinnacle of a career is to receive the Nobel prize from the hand of the King of Sweden.

Even *beauty* can lead to being honoured. Especially beautiful women are crowned as beauty queens. For one year, they are Miss Germany, Miss World, or Miss Universe, draped with the corresponding sash. In the USA in December 1999, *Lady Di* (1961–1997), the Princess of Wales, was voted to be the most beautiful woman of the century. After her fatal accident in Paris, a German magazine wrote: »The adulation of this beautiful princess, who after years of unhappiness, infidelity and bulimia had freed herself from the prison of the Windsors, transcended political and generational boundaries.«

In the various winegrowing regions of Germany, a vintage queen is crowned every year.

Practically the only car in the former DDR (German Democratic Republic) was the Trabant, an extremely basic construction with a plastic body. After the reunification of Germany (1990) this type of car almost totally disappeared off of the highway scene. Nevertheless, for nostalgic reasons, there is still an impressive number of owners. In Zwickau, the city in which the colloquially named »Trabbi« was manufactured in socialist times, a large rally of Trabant owners takes place once a year. They travel there with their converted Trabbis, decked out with special accessories. Here, too, recognition and honour play their part. Each year, the new *Trabbi-Queen* is crowned — not the most beautiful woman, but the one with the best »Trabbi-knowhow«!

During their lifetime, many rulers allowed themselves be painted by renowned artists, or modelled in particular poses, in order to erect large monuments to remind posterity of their fame.

Sometimes the urge to establish a monument to themselves is already present in people's youth. *Leonardo Di-*

Caprio (1974–), the lead actor in the 1997 *James Cameron*-produced film »Titanic«, was only just 24 years old when, in 1999, he commissioned a bronze statue of himself to sustain his likeness for posterity.
(Source: Weekly magazine with TV guide for 23–29 October accompanying *Prisma* No. 42 (1999).

Men seek glory and approval from men. Considering Romans 3:23, however, we need approval from God, not men.

A glance **at history** shows that rulers have taken names (or had them given to them) which were meant to magnify them still further. One *Gaius Oktavian* became the first Roman Emperor (Caesar), bearing the new honorific title *Augustus* (Latin: the majestic one).

Certain »add-ons« to names, such as **the Great, the Strong**, denote especial veneration and recognition. Thus we know from history:

The Greek Emperor *Alexander the Great* (BC 356-323)
The Holy Roman Emperor *Karl the Great* (742–814: *Carolus Magnus* in Latin, better known in the English-speaking world by his French title *Charlemagne*)
The Prussian King *Frederick the Great* (1712–1786).

In the city of **Brunswick**, in which I have lived since 1971, the Duke *Heinrich (Henry) the Lion* (1129/30–1185) once lived and ruled. The lion is a symbol of power and strength. Why did he not call himself *Henry the Ant*? Or *Henry the Worm*? Thus also the English King *Richard the Lionheart* (1157–1199) was not called *Richard the Chickenheart*, or *Richard the Mouseheart,* either.

From 1694–1733, *August the Strong* ruled in **Saxony**. It seems obvious why he did not call himself *August the Weak*.[12]

What the conduct of the mighty of this world shows us is that nothing can satisfy the hunger for honour and recognition. Many examples in history show us that in the course of such striving, competitors are suppressed, sidelined or even eliminated.

How will it be in Heaven in this regard? The **name of Jesus** will outshine everything. Because He is the reflection of God's glory, and the very image of God's essence, and because He has accomplished the cleansing from sins (Hebrews 1:3), »God has also highly exalted him, and given him a name which is above every name« (Philippians 2:9).

When the Bible speaks of names in this way, it has more in view than a mere label by which to call someone. There is a deeper significance behind it than when parents today call their child Kevin, Peter, Anne or Laura. With this name, the Bible also assumes sovereignty over the person to be named. What can be said about this new name?

1. The name will be new. For the word »new« Greek has two expressions: *neos* and *kainos*. *Neos* means something which is only new from the perspective of time. For instance, when a new example of something which is already

---

[12] In Saxony, actually, there was once a ruler with a very unusual name. He was called colloquially Frederick the Bitten One, and reigned as the Margrave of Meissen from 1307 to 1324. His mother fled from her spouse, who threatened her life. As an unforgettable sign she bit her son Frederick on the cheek.

known (house, chair, table) is manufactured, then this newly made item is called *neos*. The word *kainos*, on the other hand, conveys the meaning that something is not only new in time, but also in kind and character. When *Konrad Zuse* built the world's first computer in 1938, one would have used *kainos* to describe this invention in Greek. Whereas when today a computer rolls off of a manufacturer's assembly line, it is a »new« computer, but since it is an already-known item, *neos* would be the correct term.

The concept of *kainos* occurs repeatedly in Revelation: the *new* Jerusalem (3:12), the *new* song (5:9), the *new* Heaven and the *new* Earth (21:1). *Kainos* is also used in regard to our *new name* in Revelation 2:17. In Revelation 3:12 Jesus speaks of a new name which he will receive, too: »and I will write upon him the name of my God, and … *my new* [kainos] *name*.

My first name, *Werner*, appears a few hundred times in the Brunswick telephone book. Thousands of other people in various other places have the same first name. There is nothing original about it. Our heavenly name, by contrast, will be »kainos«; noone has ever had this name, and it will not occur a second time. The new name in Heaven will also remove all hunger for recognition and honour, once and for all. We will take delight in it, yet it will not cause anyone else to feel »put down«. All this is brought to expression in the picture Jesus gives of the white stone with the new name.

2. The name will aptly capture the essence of our nature:
We know of several people in the Bible whose names were altered, because there were decisive changes in their lives. The new name was an outward expression of a special promise, or a special relationship to God.

Abram became Abraham: Abram means »*high (exalted)
father*«. After his encounter with God he received a new
name: *Abraham*, which means: »father of the multitude«.
This was intended to clearly signify his new position; to
all intents he became the father of the faith.

Jacob became Israel: *Jacob* was the heel-grasper (Genesis 25:26 ff.), a deceiver and trickster. At Jabbok, Jacob
wrestled with God, and through this he came to a decisive
change in his life. After this, God gave him the name
Israel, which means: God's warrior, God's champion: he
contends for God. What a transformation!

Saul became Paul: *Saul*, the persecutor of Christians, is
converted to Jesus. He becomes a new man, *Paul*, who
becomes the greatest missionary.

When Jesus calls Peter, in John 1:42, he names him anew:
»When Jesus saw him, he said, «You are Simon son of John.
You will be called Cephas" (which, translated, is Peter [= rock]).«

When we receive a *new* (kainos!) name in Heaven, this
commences an entirely new phase of our life, namely the
one of eternal, imperishable life. We are not simply being
renamed, but rather God with this is beginning a new calling and a new history for us. A new status is established.

In Matthew 25:21 Jesus refers to this new calling, which
may not be seen in isolation from our earthly works: »Well
done, you good and faithful servant, you have been faithful over a few things, I will put you in charge of many
things; enter into the joy of your lord.«

All the things of this world are destined for destruction in eternity; in like manner, high and mighty add-ons to names, such as »the Great« or »the Strong« will vanish, along with all earthly titles of distinction. Through the new name awarded to them, all disciples of Jesus will be far more greatly honoured than all earthly titles could ever have done. When Jesus gives us this name, our person and nature could not be more fittingly characterized. With it, Jesus will express his evaluation of our worth.

3. The name will be unique: It will be a »one-off« name, not to be found again anywhere in all of Heaven. Considering that even here already, there is no repetition of the form of a snowflake or an oak leaf, and no star is exactly like any other (1 Corinthians 15:41), how much more will that be true for our names in eternity! God delights in uniqueness. We, too, have been uniquely created by God, absolutely distinct from all others. The new name will aptly describe the essence of our being.

H11: Heaven is where we become like Jesus

I hardly dare to say it, but it is written in 1 John 3:2: »Dear friends, now we are children of God, and what we will be has not yet been made known. But we know that when he appears, **we shall be like him**.«

What does that mean? Man was created in the image of God, but this identity was lost in the Fall. The Bible is referring to Jesus when it says that, »the Son is the radiance of God's glory and the exact representation of his being« (Hebrews 1:3). If in heaven we become like Jesus, then we too will be the radiance of God's glory and the exact representation of His being.

Individually, we will have our unique personalities, but our qualitative physical traits (beauty, glory, figure, physical perfection) will be that of Jesus (Philippians 3:21). That body will not be restricted by time or space (John 20:19).

Here on Earth, it is very rare that we meet someone who shares our thoughts and beliefs. But when this does happen, we cherish these conversations and time seems to fly. That which is said is stimulating and enriching, usually leading us to new discoveries which we would not have made but for the other person's input.

In heaven, we will become one in thought with Jesus. Communication with Him will be an integral creative element. Even after all of our earthly questions have been answered, there will still be new and boundless things to contemplate. Just like the way that those dear to us want to get to know us as well as possible, we will want to get to know the inexhaustible kingdom of God (Isaiah 40:28) and Jesus (Colossians 2:3). Right after the creation of man, God gave him the creative task of naming the animals (Genesis 2:19-20). Does it not follow that the Lord in heaven will continue this creative conversation? Communication in heaven is not an exchange of knowledge with which we could fill an encyclopedia, but a continually enriching dialogue.

H12: Heaven is something special to look forward to

In looking at the content of Jesus' words, one aspect is impossible to ignore. He continually invites us to heaven. He began His preaching with the words, »the time has come. The kingdom of God is near. Repent and believe the good news« (Mark 1:15). Jesus tried to describe heaven to us in many parables. »The kingdom of heaven is like

- »a man who sowed good seed in his field« (Matthew 13:24).
- »a mustard seed« (Matthew 13:31).
- »yeast« (Matthew 13:33).
- »treasure hidden in a field« (Matthew 13:44).
- »a merchant looking for fine pearls (Matthew 13:45).
- »a net« (Matthew 13:47).
- »a king who prepared a wedding banquet for his son« (Matthew 22:2).

The soul-searching conversation with Zacchaeus ends with a reference to eternal salvation: »Today salvation has come to this house. ... For the Son of Man came to seek and to save what is lost« (Luke 19:9-10).

Jesus does not promise children an easy life on this earth, but he promises them heaven: »Let the little children come to me, and do not hinder them, for the kingdom of God belongs to such as these« (Luke 18:16).

When Jesus sees the paralytic he does not tell him first »Get up and walk!«, but »Your sins are forgiven« (Matthew 9:2). It is once again clear that a decisive freedom from sin is a prerequisite for heaven, and is of the utmost importance to Jesus.

The Sermon on the Mount is so often misquoted today, but heaven is its main subject:

- »Blessed are those who are persecuted because of righteousness, for theirs is the kingdom of heaven« (Matthew 5:10).
- »But seek first his kingdom and his righteousness and all these things will be given to you as well« (Matthew 6:33).

- »Enter through the narrow gate. For wide is the gate
  and broad is the road that leads to destruction, and
  many enter through it. But small is the gate and narrow the road that leads to life, and only a few find it«
  (Matthew 7:13-14).

As the disciples returned from a missionary journey, they
rejoiced to know that even the demons submitted to them.
Jesus reminded them that they had a much greater reason to rejoice, »Do not rejoice that the spirits submit to
you, but rejoice that your names are written in heaven«
(Luke 10:20). Jesus gives absolute priority to this particular reason for joy. 1 Peter 1:8 refers to this rejoicing
»with joy unspeakable and full of glory«.

If we show the way to glory to just one other person, it
will result in overwhelming joy in heaven: »In the same
way, I tell you, there is rejoicing in the presence of the
angels of God over one sinner who repents« (Luke 15:10).

This means:

- The most important task God's children have is to
  spread the Word that will lead people to heaven. This
  heavenly assignment still has utmost priority.

- Until the return of Jesus, the eternal goal must remain
  the main topic of biblical preaching and pastoral care.

- Knowing that we have a home in heaven (Philippians
  3:20) should form the substance of our lives and infect
  others with our joy.

Bibliography

[B1]   Bauch, A., Fischer, B., Heindorff, T., Schröder, R: Performance of the PTB reconstructed primary clock CS1 and an estimate of its current uncertainty. *Metrologia* (1998), **35**:829 - 845

[B2]   Boschke, F. L: Und 1000 Jahre sind wie ein Tag. – Die Zeit, das unverstandene Phänomen – Knaur, 1st edition 1979, 223 pp.

[C1]   Clairon, A., Laurent, P., Santarelli, G., Ghezalli, S., Lea, S. N., Bahoura, M: A Cesium Fountain Frequency Standard: Preliminary Results. *IEEE, Transactions on Instrumentation and Measurement* (1995), **44**:128-131.

[D1]   Davies, P: About Time – Einstein's unfinished revolution. Simon and Schuster. New York (1995).

[F1]   Feynman, R. P: The Character of Physical Law. The MIT Press, 2nd Edition 1995, 173 pp.

[G1]   Gitt, W: In the Beginning was Information CLV Bielefeld, 1st English edition 1997, 256 pp. (3th German edition 2001, 288 pp.)

[G2]   Gitt, W: Questions I Have Always Wanted to Ask CLV Bielefeld, 2nd English edition 1998, 192 pp. (17th German edition 2000, 190 pp.)

[G3]   Gitt, W: Stars and their Purpose: Signposts in Space. CLV Bielefeld, 1st English edition 1996, 217 pp. (3rd German edition 1999, 222 pp.)

[G4]   Gitt, W: In sechs Tagen vom Chaos zum Menschen - Logos oder Chaos; Naturwissenschaftliche und bibli-

sche Grundfragen zur Schöpfung; Aussagen und Ein-
wände zur Evolutionslehre - Hänssler-Verlag, Neu-
hausen-Stuttgart, 5th Edition, 1998, 237 pp.

[G5]   Gitt, W: Was ist Zeit, und was ist Ewigkeit? *Astrono-
mie + Raumfahrt 36*(2):6-19 (1999).

[G6]   Gitt, W: Ist Information eine Eigenschaft der Mate-
rie? Westdeutscher Verlag, EuS **9**(2):205-207 (1998).

[G7]   Gitt, W: The Wonder of Man. CLV Bielefeld, 1st
English edition 1999, 156 pp. (1st German edition
1996, 141 pp.)

[K1]   Kemner, H: Jesus trifft dich überall. Brunnenverlag,
Gießen, Basel, 1971, 80 pp.

[K2]   Kunsch, K: Der Mensch in Zahlen. Gustav Fischer
Verlag, Stuttgart, Jena, Lübeck, Ulm, 1997, 344 pp.

[M1]   Mettler, M: The Art of Having Time. *Cross Talk,
The Magazine for European Business Flyers,* February
1999, pp. 32-33.

[M2]   Muschalek, M: Gottbekenntnisse moderner Natur-
forscher. Morus-Verlag, Berlin, 4h edition 1964, 296
pp.

[S1]   Seydel, R., Meier, B: Romy Schneider – Ein Leben
in Bildern. Henschel Verlag, Berlin, 1996, 344 pp.

[S2]   Sobel, D: Longitude: The true story of a lone genius
who solved the greatest scientific problem of his time.
Walker Publishing Company, Inc., 1995.

[X1]   SI-System: Das internationale Einheitensystem (SI).
Friedr. Vieweg & Sohn, Braunschweig, 1982, 66 pp.

Other Books written by Prof. Dr. Werner Gitt

Questions I have always wanted to ask

2nd English edition 1998, 192 pp.,

In Germany the book is in its 17th edition (2000). The book is available in 15 languages: Bulgarian, Croatian, Czech, English, Finnish, French, German, Hungarian, Italian, Lithuanian, Kirghizian, Polish, Romanian, Spain, Russian.

Sooner or later everyone, whether defending the Christian faith or just taking an interest in it, comes face to face with a number of crucial basic questions. The author, a prominent scientist and evangelist who has spoken to many thousands of people across the world, has heard the same sorts of questions from virtually every person who claims to be searching for God. These questions have now been brought together in this book and concisely answered.

But this is not the 'standard' sort of question/answer book which Christian 'insiders' might expect. All the questions it deals with are real – they were actually asked by someone. So this is not some collection of hair-splitting theological or theoretical concepts. Rather, it is a book which tries to address head-on those vital issues on the minds of all who are doubting, questioning and searching (not to mention a few of the more unusual queries the author has come across).

If Animals Could Talk

2nd English edition 1999, 132 pp.,

In Germany the book is in its 12th edition (2000). The book is available in 13 languages: Bulgarian, Chinese, Croatian, Czech, English, Estonian, French, German, Hungarian, Polish, Romanian, Spain, Russian.

Animals have very efficient communication systems, which they use to converse with one another. Nevertheless, they cannot speak to us in human language. The authors have taken it upon themselves to act as their verbal representatives. The animals take up several possible questions and deal with them in this imaginary conversation. The authors have in this way kept the content narrative lively and entertaining – without forfeiting scientific credibility.
This book has something for everyone, both young and not so young, experts and laymen alike.

Did God Use Evolution?

1st English edition 1993, 152 pp.,

In Germany the book is in its 6th edition (1999). The book is available in 5 languages: Czech, English, German, Hungarian, Russian.

Many well-known scientists are turning away from the synthetic theory of evolution in favour of a doctrine of theistic evolution. The reason for this trend is obvious, because no natural process has ever been observed where information originated spontaneously in matter.
It was hoped to close this gap by reverting to theistic evolu-

tion. According to this view God started the process of evolution and guided and steered it over millions of years. This idea has gained some popularity amongst Christians.

As an information scientist Werner Gitt critically analyses and rejects the assumptions and consequences of the doctrine of theistic evolution. His conclusions are fresh and startling.

In the Beginning was Information

1st English edition 1997, 256 pp.,

In Germany the book is in its 2nd edition (1994). The book is available in 3 languages: English, German, Hungarian.

What does the migratory flight of the golden plover have in common with a postcard? What is the common factor between a computer program and hieroglyphics? And what property is shared between the processes taking place in living cells and the message of the Bible? The distinctive common quantity in all these cases is information.

All living organisms require information to function. If we want to make meaningful and useful statements about the origin of life, then we first have to explain what information is and how it came about. The author of this book uses many illustrative and striking examples to clarify this question. The basic principles of information are clearly established in terms of laws of nature which are just as valid and applicable as those employed in the natural sciences. The current materialistic representations of information are criticised, and a new model for the origin of life is derived.

In this book the author describes a new way of understanding creation and the Bible.

The Wonder of Man

1st English edition 1999, 156 pp.,

In Germany the book is in its 1st edition (1996). The book is available in 3 languages: English, German, Russian.

In *The Wonder of Man* you will find many remarkable details about what it is that makes up you, a human being. Who wouldn't be amazed to find out, for example, that:

- We don't actually hear with two ears, but with six. Not only does this help us orientate ourselves in space, it's why we can pay attention to just one conversation in a room full of people talking at once.
- The optic nerve, the 'information connection' from the eye to the brain, is only 2 mm thick, but contains more than one million nerve fibres, all insulated from each other. Even in our modern age of glass fibre connections, communications engineers can only dream of having a 'cable' with such high-tech capacities.
- We can normally distinguish between around 10,000 various smells, but even this remarkable ability can be greatly enhanced with practice, as in the case of professional wine and coffee tasters.
- Your heart beats 100,000 times in a day, and pumps enough blood in your lifetime to fill a huge skyscraper. In every drop of your blood there are 250 million red blood cells; the number of these cells in all the blood in your body is an unimaginable 250,000,000,000,000!

· Our brain consists of around 100 billion nerve cells, around the same order of magnitude as the number of stars in our Milky Way galaxy. The length of the nerve fibres in the cerebrum alone, laid end to end, would reach much further than the distance from the earth to the moon.

The above small sample gives a glimpse of the many unique features of our design and construction. These are expounded in detail in this book, making its title *The Wonder of Man* particularly appropriate.

Having given many amazing medical, physical, chemical and information-theoretical details of the way we are made, the author does not, however, leave it at that, but draws logical conclusions from these about the Originator of mankind. He concerns himself with the question of how we stand in our Creator's sight, and what our destiny is. The aspect of our having been made for eternity is dealt with in appropriate depth.

This book is not aimed at any special group of readers, but at everyone capable of fascination and wonder, and interested in the discovery of new things. Thus both lay and specialist/technical readers will find themselves catered for within these pages.

Stars and their Purpose: Signposts in Space

1st English edition 1996, 217 pp.,

In Germany the book is in its 3nd edition (1999). The book is available in 5 languages: Chinese, English, German, Hungarian, Russian.

What expectations do you have when you start reading a book with the title "Signposts in Space"? Perhaps you think of the "little green men" which Bell and Hewish discovered when they first received signals from pulsars? Or maybe you're interested in reading something about intelligent life forms, whose existence in distant galaxies provides the material for much speculations?
Rather, in this book, we'll be looking at the effect which star systems have on us humans beings. We shall answer questions which are as fascinating as they are fundamental: What are the origins of the universe? Is its existence a coincidence or does it have pre-destined design? Why are there stars in the enormous universe? Who is their creator? What was the star of Bethlehem? Is it possible to have a personal relationship with the creator?
The starry sky is there for everyone and can be seen from every point on the earth. Thus this impressive scenery invites us to spend some time in reflection.

What About the Other Religions?

1st English edition 1995, 159 pp.,

In Germany the book is in its 6th edition (1997). The book is available in 6 languages: Czech, English, German, Hungarian, Polish, Russian.

This book deals with a topic which often leads to heated discussions:

- There are so many religions. Are they all wrong, is there only a single correct one, or do all ultimately lead to the same goal?
- People with other religions are honest in their beliefs. They perform their prayers and sacrifices sincerely and trust fully in their religion. Surely God must also see it that way. If God is a God of love, must He not recognise all efforts to reach Him?
- Our times are characterised by understanding and tolerance. Shouldn't that also be the case between religions, as *Frederick the Great* (1712-1786) already believed: "Everyone should be saved in his own manner?" Isn't the Gospel highly intolerant, if it throws out all other ways and claims to be uniquely correct?

These are among the questions most often asked during discussions about faith. We need real answers to help us out. The author provides a thorough, Biblically-based work, which allows one to orient himself in this field of conflict.

CREATION MAGAZINE

The easy way to stay up to date on creation and evolution.

Creation *magazine – 56 full-colour, glossy pages packed with beautifully-illustrated, well-written articles that reveal the truth about origins. Encourages your faith while it helps you to defend it (1 Peter 3:15).*

Readers in over 120 countries enjoy this quality magazine. As a subscriber, you receive an attractive new edition every 13 weeks, and discounts on many advertised books.

- **The latest evidences against evolution.**
- **No paid advertising.**
- **Articles written by experts for all ages.**
- **Powerful evidences for creation.**

Send for your first thrilling issue today!

SUBSCRIPTION PRICES

AUSTRALIA		CANADA (CAN$)	
1 year (4 issues)	A$25	1 year (4 issues)	$29.95
2 years (8 issues)	A$47	2 years (8 issues)	$57
3 years (12 issues)	A$67	3 years (12 issues)	$84

NEW ZEALAND		SOUTH AFRICA	
1 year (4 issues)	NZ$32	1 year (4 issues)	R110
2 years (8 issues)	NZ$62	2 years (8 issues)	R210
3 years (12 issues)	NZ$89	3 years (12 issues)	R300

UK/EUROPE		**SINGAPORE**	
1 year (4 issues)	£12.95	1 year (4 issues)	S$32
2 years (8 issues)	£25	2 years (8 issues)	S$62
3 years (12 issues)	£37	3 years (12 issues)	S$89

USA		OTHER COUNTRIES	
1 year (4 issues)	US$22	1 year (4 issues)	A$29
2 years (8 issues)	US$42	2 years (8 issues)	A$56
3 years (12 issues)	US$60	3 years (12 issues)	A$83

Where can I get more information?

Internationally: <www.AnswersInGenesis.org> (including on-line bookstore)

AUSTRALIA
Answers in Genesis,
PO Box 6302,
Acacia Ridge DC, Qld 4110
Phone: (07) 3273 7650
Fax: (07) 3273 7672
ABN 31 010 120 304

USA
Answers in Genesis,
PO Box 6330,
Florence, Kentucky 41022
Phone: (859) 727 2222
Fax: (859) 727 2299

NEW ZEALAND
Answers in Genesis,
PO Box 39005,
Howick 1730, Auckland
Phone/Fax: (09) 537 4818
A Registered
Charitable Trust

CANADA
Answers in Genesis,
5-420 Erb Street West,
Suite 213,
Waterloo, ON N2L 6K6
Phone: (519) 746-7616
Fax: (519) 746-7617

UK/EUROPE
Answers in Genesis,
PO Box 5262,
Leicester LE2 3XU, UK
Phone: (0116) 270 8400
Fax: (0116) 270 0110
Registered
Charity No. 102 4543

OTHER COUNTRIES
Answers in Genesis,
PO Box 6302,
Acacia Ridge, Qld 4110,
Australia
Phone: +617 3273 7650
Fax: +617 3273 7672

The above books by Dr Gitt in English
may be ordered from:

Christliche Literatur-Verbreitung • P.O. Box 11 01 35
D-33661 Bielefeld • GERMANY
++49 - 521 - 9 47 24 13 (Voice) • 9 47 24 23 (Fax)
http://www.clv.de (Internet) • *order@clv.de* (eMail)
or see: www.AnswersInGenesis.org